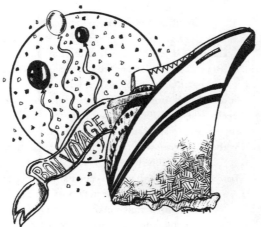

PERSONAL TRAVEL DIARY
by Bob Schoolsky

Longmeadow Press

CONTENTS

ACKNOWLEDGMENTS

For various reasons certain individuals unknowingly supplied input over the years helpful in compiling this book. Carm Tintle of Banfi Vintners, a world traveler who manages to maintain his wry sense of humor under the most trying conditions; Fran Skurka Garcia, an enthusiastic teacher who will take off for anywhere at the click of a luggage clasp; and Bunny Blane, the world's best travel agent and travel companion.

—*Robert Schoolsky*

"Much have I travell'd in the realms of gold . . ."
                                        John Keats

INTRODUCTION

Now that NASA is accepting applications for space travel from ordinary citizens, the universe is your oyster. For the less adventurous, the travel industry has arranged trips and tours for neophytes striking out for the first time, and for globe-trotting veterans. Wherever your destination, this book is designed to go with you on your travels. With it tucked in your pocket you won't have to search for needed information, reference numbers, and important points that will help to ensure a carefree vacation. We've planned this book for the vacation-bound as well as for the seasoned business traveler. But remember, regardless of the purpose of your trip, there is no better recipe for youthful spirits, open-mindedness and continual pleasure than that which travel offers. Bon voyage!

CURRENCY EXCHANGE

In recent years the value of the U.S. dollar versus foreign currency has fluctuated according to market demands. Since experts are often wrong about the direction of the dollar at any given time, it is unwise to try to second-guess the professionals. Exchange rates posted in your daily newspaper are bulk rates for trading purposes and differ from retail rates.

Try to make all of your purchases with credit cards. The credit card company will convert your purchase at the favorable bulk rate, probably saving you money. Use of credit cards also means carrying fewer traveler's checks or less cash. European countries have highly sophisticated terminals at hotels, shops, and gas stations that simplify the use of "plastic." VISA and American Express are the most commonly accepted cards.

If possible, convert currency at a bank or an American Express office. The exception is bank counters at air terminals. Rates at those facilities are not as good as the same bank's downtown office. Hotels and stores will add a surcharge. However, unlike shops in the U.S., foreign stores, in the smallest towns and villages, have instant access, via computer, to daily rates in all currencies. Exchange is not a problem.

Except in an emergency, do not convert funds when banks are closed; plan ahead. Do not convert U.S. cash. The rate for "greenbacks" is usually a point or two lower than for traveler's checks. The difference is usually posted on the rate board.

Unless you live in a major metropolitan area, you will find that local banks in the United States are not geared to convert funds. Even if they have an inventory of foreign currency on hand, the rate will not be favorable. Investigate the purchase of foreign traveler's checks. It pays to carry them in addition to U.S. fund checks. You should purchase a small amount of foreign cash and currency in advance. Exchange will be relatively expensive, but the cash will come in handy on arrival for immediate expenses such as porter tipping.

TRAVEL AGENTS

AGENT FEES

Surprisingly, a large segment of the public has never utilized a travel agent. Many people who utilize the services of an agent for business travel use the "do it yourself" approach when planning a vacation.

Much of this results from a misunderstanding of the services an agent can render and the cost involved. Today, with hundreds of vacation options available and countless fare variations offered by scheduled airlines, it pays to seek the services of a professional.

Retail travel agencies earn commissions from the vendor selling the service. They get from 8 percent to 20 percent, depending on the nature of the service, and the vendor's arrangements. Normally, there will be no charge to you for the agent's services. They can often save you money by seeking out the lowest fares. However, should you need an F.I.T. (Foreign Inclusive Tour), involving lengthy planning sessions and conferences, you should expect to pay a consulting fee.

If you are planning a tour that involves a number of different hotel reservations, and one or more does not have a U.S. representative, you should expect to pay for necessary letters, overseas phone calls, cables and/or telex charges. In situations where hotels do not pay a commission, many agents will charge a fee reflecting the amount of work involved and the overall value of your bookings.

SELECTING AND DEALING WITH AN AGENT

Unfortunately, there is little regulation of travel agents on a state, federal, or industry basis. Agents are not required to meet any educational requirements, and except for minimum financial standards set by the airlines—for their protection, not yours—they can operate on a shoestring. Membership in a national or regional trade organization is not necessarily a guarantee of quality or reliability.

The best recommendation is from a friend who has dealt with a particular agent or agency. If you wish, call the local Better Business Bureau and ask if there have been any complaints registered about the agent, and inquire at the consumer affairs department in your city or the state attorney's office for additional information.

Determine if your agent has visited the destination you have selected and has stayed at a particular hotel. Agents have extensive trade publications on hand with detailed descriptions of hotels and cities, but a personal experience is always better.

An agency will sometimes be a member of a consortium. This affords them a certain degree of leverage in setting commission rates and bonus overrides with a particular vendor because of volume. If you can, determine if this is the reason an airline, car rental, hotel, or package tour is being recommended.

Selecting a travel agent to assist you in planning and booking a cruise is most important. This is the one area of travel that requires a great deal of expertise. Considering the total cost and the fact that you are placing all of your vacation eggs in one basket, you should consider using a specialist.

A good agent will have sailed on a number of cruises and be familiar with the various itineraries offered. Most important, an agent that specializes in cruising will often book a number of cabins in advance, at special rates, and thus can offer reduced fares to clients. Unlike other types of travel, discounting, sometimes amounting to cash savings of a thousand dollars or more, is prevalent in the cruise business.

Agents who sell a set number of reservations often receive bonus staterooms which they can sell or keep for personal use. Many agencies will sell these cabins at steep discounts. Check the advertisements in your local newspaper's travel section.

The closer to the sailing date, the greater your leverage with the agent or cruise line that still has unsold cabins in their inventory. If you seek bargains and are prepared to travel on a few days' notice, you can often strike a good deal. Conversely, if you book far enough in advance, with payment in full, many lines will offer a good discount from the listed fare.

Make sure your agent provides all financial arrangements in writing. This is particularly important in the area concerning penalty fees. Make sure you receive an invoice and/or a receipt. Penalty fees should be clearly stated on your receipt. Carefully read all "terms and conditions" statements on brochures and flyers prior to making a reservation. Check out the reputation of tour operators and vendors with local regulatory agencies.

PAYMENT

Airline tickets usually must be paid at the time of ticketing. Tours and packages will require a deposit with additional payments scheduled at specific times. Hotels often require one night's deposit. These terms are set by various vendors and tour operators. Agents do not have any flexibility in this regard and must submit the amount of payment called for at the time of reservation.

Agents can offer credit-card charging only if this method of payment is offered by the vendor. Usually, all scheduled airline tickets can be charged. If you desire extended payments on an American Express, Diner's Club or Carte Blanche charge, you must state this fact and check the charge slip before signing. Credit card firms do not allow any retroactive changes.

INSURANCE

Most credit cards provide some type of liability and life insurance when tickets are charged on the card. However, coverage rarely extends to baggage or trip cancellation. Both types of insurance are strongly recommended and can be purchased through your travel agent.

TRAVEL DOCUMENTS

Your agent should deliver three sets of documents prior to departure.

1. Your tickets: Check carefully for flight numbers, arrival and departure times. Call immediately if there are errors.

2. Travel vouchers for all ground reservations: Each voucher should give the name and address of the hotel or service, your name, dates of arrival and departure, exact description and nature of reservation, rate in U.S. or local funds, amount of deposit, if any. The voucher should be presented at the time of arrival.

3. Three copies of your complete itinerary: One to take with you and one each for your home and office. The itinerary should duplicate the voucher information, with airport or pier check-in

times, arrival times, meals served en route, hotel phone numbers, FAX numbers, Telex numbers, and cable codes.

Your agent should also furnish you with specific hints and tips, dining and shopping suggestions, sightseeing guides, and general touring material on each destination. Remember, however, even the most competent agent cannot promise or guarantee that you will not be pinched in Rome, insulted in Paris, or get sick in Mexico.

JET LAG

Fight the urge to get into bed on arrival at the hotel. Quickly unpack (if your room is available), or check your baggage with the porter. Get out on the town. Do some easy sightseeing, some shopping, generally get the "feel" of the city. Have a light dinner and retire early. You'll be the better for it the next day.

DUTY-FREE SHOPPING

To a large extent the bargains of yesteryear simply no longer exist at airport duty-free shops. The discounts or savings are often no different than those found in your own home town at a large volume retailer who works on minimum markups. The savings on American brand cigarettes, for example, may only be a dollar or two. Often, you can do better on the plane when the so-called duty-free shop opens shortly before arrival.

The best bargains in spirits are usually among the specialty items such as liqueurs and aperitifs. Some of these items, tasted overseas for the first time, may not be available in your local shop. Unless you have been fortunate enough to purchase a rare old bottle, most wines can be purchased for less at home.

Be careful when buying electronic goods. Be sure the voltage requirements are equivalent to those in the United States and check whether the same warranties and guaranties are as good as those offered at home. The best thing to do is prepare a shopping list in advance, listing the discount prices at home for comparison purposes.

MEDICAL CONSIDERATIONS

There are few places in the world that still require immunization shots. Your physician will be helpful in this regard. Be sure he gives you a record of any shots or boosters. You should also secure copies of prescriptions you use in case you need the medication. A brief written statement on treatment of any preexisting conditions would also be helpful.

PASSPORTS AND VISAS

The U.S. Passport Agency maintains offices in all major cities. Applications and information for securing your passport by mail can be obtained at some local post offices. Allow sufficient time for processing. Emergency service is available at an additional fee. Overseas, lost or stolen passports should be reported immediately to the nearest U.S. embassy or consulate. Your passport number should be recorded and kept separately.

It is wise to check with the advisory service of the U.S. State Department (listed under U.S. Government in the telephone directory) for any tourist alerts.

Few countries require visas for U.S. citizens. Some insist on passports while others only require proof of U.S. citizenship in the form of a copy of a birth certificate or voter registration card. Currently, France is the only major Western European nation that requires visas. The same visa is required for French possessions in the West Indies. Visa applications must be made to a country's embassy, consulate, or tourist board. Your travel agent will have the necessary forms and can assist you. A fee is charged, and passport-type photographs generally are required.

FOREIGN CUSTOMS

For the most part, you need not concern yourself with foreign customs, unless you are bringing in a gift to a resident of the country, or are carrying alcohol or tobacco products exceeding allowable limits. Many countries have regulations regarding the amounts of their currency that can be brought in or removed. Check in advance if in doubt. Be sure that you have all your drugs in prescription containers and have prescriptions for them.

UNITED STATES CUSTOMS

Even the most honest traveler gets nervous facing a customs officer. Don't get tongue-tied when asked about the value or origin of an object fished from the bottom of a suitcase. A customs declaration will be handed to you before landing or disembarking. If the value of gifts and purchases does not exceed the current exemption, merely fill in the identification portion at the top of the form.

Depending on where you visited, you are allowed to bring in a specified quantity of duty-free alcohol and tobacco products. Don't bring back any fresh fruit, plants, flowers, fresh pork or meat products, or certain dairy products. Keep all receipts handy for reference and proof of payment. Try to pack all purchases in one bag.

Families traveling together can group purchases. If the total exceeds the current maximum, you must itemize on the back of the form. The customs officer will usually calculate duty, if any, on items carrying the lowest rate—at wholesale cost. Personal checks will be accepted for duty payments.

VALUE ADDED TAX (VAT)

A consumption, sales, or internal duty tax with rates varying from country to country and from product to product. Some stores will permit you to group purchases to achieve required minimums, allowing claim of refund of all or a portion of the tax. The store will prepare the form. Present it at the designated customs location before leaving the country.

You may be required to present the item for inspection, so have it available. Leave sufficient time for this procedure. Refunds should reach you in six weeks. If paying by credit card, see if the store will fill out a credit slip at the time of purchase. The refund will be credited on your monthly statement, often in the same month as the charge.

DEPARTURE TAX

Many countries charge a departure and/or arrival tax or airport fee. This is usually not included in the cost of your plane ticket. Check with your travel agent and be prepared to pay it on arrival or departure.

GETTING AROUND LIKE A NATIVE

TELEPHONES

Many hotels, here and abroad, impose a surcharge that can often double or triple the cost of the call. Some hotels, even in the U.S., have surcharges on local calls. Check hotel policy. You can often save on these charges if you have a telephone credit card, or if you call collect.

Some hotels have joined "Teleplan," which eliminates surcharges when calls are direct dialed. An alternative: Place calls from telephone centers, post offices, railroad stations, or airports. Generally, all have attendants on hand to help you with your call, and do not impose surcharges.

All countries, including the U.S., have a country code that must be dialed or given to the operator, unless the number called is within the same country. In addition, there is a region or city code, similar to our area codes. These numbers can be omitted if calling within the same city or region.

TRANSPORTATION OPTIONS

Foreign air fares are very expensive, since the airlines are usually state-owned, with no competition. The cost of air travel from one city or country to another can exceed the cost of a transatlantic flight. However, if you plan to visit a number of countries, you should investigate the cost of buying a tour package from a travel agent at your first destination. Overseas agents may offer low-cost package tours.

Train service is often modern, speedy, and much cheaper than air transportation. Three classes of travel are usually offered, and second or third class is often a viable option, though the seat may be harder, and there may be more people in a compartment than first class. Generally, the cost of a ticket does not include a reserved seat. There are additional charges for seat reservations.

On-board meals can range from haute cuisine to cafeteria-style service. If you intend to do a great deal of train travel in Europe, consider purchasing a Eurorail pass. They are good for three months and provide unlimited train travel in Europe. These tickets must be purchased in the United States.

In-city metro or bus service is usually very reliable. Easy-to-read maps and graphic signs make it almost impossible to get lost. Check in advance to find out when service shuts down at night, so that you are not stranded.

Taxi drivers are the same all over the world. Don't be surprised to find the mirror image of the good and bad in your own home town. A driver's refusal to take you to a certain destination may be backed by regulation. There may be surcharges during certain hours, particularly at night when public transportation stops. It is all quite legal. Such surcharges, in addition to the meter total, must be posted in the cab.

RESTAURANTS AND FOOD

Most establishments include taxes and a service charge that ranges from 10 percent to 15 percent and will so state on the menu and on the check. If the food and service have been particularly good, it is customary to leave a little extra. If the service charge is not included, tip as you would at home. If there is a wine steward, figure on 10 percent of the cost of all wine ordered. Bear in mind that bottled water in restaurants can be expensive. There may be a "bread and butter" fee or cover charge.

Many countries rate the quality or level of their restaurants, and this rating is displayed at the entrance. Menus are often required to be posted in the window for decision-making before entering. In some cases, restaurants must provide a minimum, fixed-price, tourist meal. This must be posted and supplied on request. In some countries, Japan for instance, fast food establishments will have mockups of all menu selections in the window to entice you, giving you an idea of how the dish is made.

Try to arrange for at least one picnic lunch. It is not only fun and inexpensive but also gives you the opportunity to shop in a local market, getting the taste and feel of the region.

ADDITIONAL GRATUITIES

It always pays to have a supply of small bills and change in your pocket or purse to take care of many of the tipping situations that pop up during the day. They are subject to local custom, but by learning the rules you will establish your credentials as a travel veteran. Restroom attendants expect a tip and can often be visibly annoyed if ignored. Theater ushers who show you to your seat should receive a few coins.

A tip should be given to the doorman if he calls a cab for you, opens a door, or assists you with packages when you return from a shopping spree. The chambermaid should be tipped at the end of your stay. Generally, you should plan on leaving the equivalent of two U.S. dollars per person for each night of your stay. If you are in a very expensive establishment, or if the maid renders a special service, tip accordingly.

In England, and some other countries, hotels employ a hall porter on each floor. He will generally be the one to bring tea or coffee at odd hours and perform other services. He should be tipped accordingly.

The concierge usually has his own desk or station and, depending on the size of the hotel, may have a number of assistants. He should be tipped before departure, unless you have taken care of his gratuity each time he performs a service for you. Upon request, the concierge will make restaurant and theater reservations, direct you to specific stores for certain gift items, arrange for sightseeing tours, make plane and train reservations and reserve rooms for you at your next destination. Remember that for many services, particularly in the case of theater tickets or sightseeing tours, it is normal to pay him in full. He will give you a voucher for the service arranged.

IN-FLIGHT TIPS

Avoid alcoholic beverages.
Drink water and/or juice as often as possible.
Eat as little as possible, unless you are very hungry.
Familiarize yourself with emergency life-saving equipment.
Keep seat belt loosely buckled when seated.
Note the nearest emergency exit.
Replace your shoes with soft slippers for comfort.
Try not to be a "clock-watcher."
Walk up and down the aisle occasionally.
If your ears are affected by pressure changes, take a deep breath, hold it, pinch your nostrils, and *gently* try to blow air through your nose until you feel a slight "pop" in the ears. Swallowing large gulps of air is an alternative procedure.
If you experience nausea, take anti-nausea pills and alert the attendant.
If you have any special medical needs, be certain the attendant is aware of them before you take off.

SHIPBOARD TIPS

Acquaint yourself with the steward most responsible for your cabin area.
Familiarize yourself with emergency evacuation procedures.
Know where the doctor on the ship is located.

If you have any special medical needs, be certain the steward and, if necessary, the doctor, know about them.

If you experience seasickness, take anti-nausea medicine and alert the proper ship's staff members.

SOME FINAL WORDS OF WISDOM

Remember, even though you're on vacation, everyone around you is putting in a regular day's work. If the taxi driver doesn't speak English, shouting or speaking very slowly will not surmount the language barrier. Try writing your destination.

Knowledgeable travelers never get upset about things that are beyond their control. The traveler with the most passport entries is never irritated when, arriving dead tired, looking forward to a luxurious bath, he or she finds the room is still occupied. Or perhaps the room is ready, but the shower turns out to be a tiled phone booth with or without a shower curtain around it, and the shower head resembles the receiver of a 19th-century telephone normally found in stylish bordellos.

Maybe the shower/bath controls are so modern and complicated it requires an astronaut training program to operate them. Or, the tub is the size of a postage stamp that can barely accommodate a rubber duck. If the advertised "air conditioning" is a semi-cool draft, barely noticeable, accept the fact that the locals don't keep temperatures set at the level of a meat locker.

There are other items that will probably occur and should also be ignored. For instance, your plane arrives at or leaves from the gate farthest from the terminal, especially when there is a porter strike, and you have to carry all of your luggage. Or when you arrive at the airport with time to spare, the flight will be two hours late.

Contrary to the laws of logic, luggage checked last will be the last on the conveyer belt on arrival. The most interesting sights will always be on the other side of the plane, train or bus. In flight, the moment you go to the lavatory, the "Fasten Seat Belt" sign will go on. When the pilot announces a "ten-minute delay" in landing, he really means "if we are fired out of a cannon and have a strong tailwind."

Finally, the drapes in your hotel room will close except for the last half-inch, which will give you an excellent view of sunrise at 5:30 A.M.

LUXURY ON THE BOUNDING MAIN

Vacations afloat are the fastest-growing segment of the travel business. The reasons for this popularity are not difficult to understand, since cruising provides all of the elements of adventure and escape that most of us seek when planning our vacations.

Cruise lines, recognizing the potential in this vast market, have maintained an ambitious program of constructing new state-of-the-art vessels every year. These "Sea Queens," with added features and exotic destinations, are designed to whet the interest of veteran mariners as well as those embarking on their first voyage. Cruising has changed considerably over the years, with the emphasis on comfort.

The rigid caste systems that ruled social life on the grand ocean liners of yesteryear began to disappear when ships shed their traditional role as strictly transportation from one continent or port to another. Few vessels still maintain the three-class method of segregating travelers: first, cabin, and tourist.

Today, the accent is on recreation. The liners are floating luxury hotel/resorts with open facilities and haute cuisine menus available to all passengers, regardless of the type of their accommodations. For the most part, fares depend on the size and luxury of cabin or stateroom accommodations, the deck level, length of cruise, and special services provided.

For more information on selecting an agent to help you plan your cruise, see the section about agents in Travel Tips.

SELECTING A CRUISE

The world is your oyster. At latest count there are over 150 major cruise ships covering the seven seas offering trips as short as a few days to 'round-the-world journeys lasting six months or more. The longer cruises can often be booked in segments, so that you can join the trip at a foreign destination and leave at another port.

Many lines offer "Fly and Sail" packages for this purpose. The air fares in these packages are extremely reasonable and cannot be equaled if booked alone.

In addition to the major vessels, hundreds of smaller ships sail the larger lakes, rivers, and inland waterways here and abroad. You can opt for the ultimate in luxury or get the feel of the sea and the wind in your face on a working schooner as part of the crew.

THEME CRUISES

A recent survey of the types of theme cruises indicates that almost every special-interest area and avocation is catered to. Some of the more esoteric examples include: archaeology, cinematography, computers, geology, political science, and zoology.

These cruises feature special shipboard activities and shore excursions built around designated themes. Experts and specialists in the field are on board to lecture and conduct classes. Be sure to read all printed material on the cruise and ask questions of your travel agent, or contact the line directly to determine the amount of time allotted.

Some cruises will feature a theme, but only schedule one or two events. The "guest expert" or announced "talent" may join the cruise at a foreign port and give one or two lectures or talks. If your intent is to increase your knowledge on a specific subject, be sure the cruise satisfies your requirements.

Good sources for information on special theme cruises are museums' membership organizations, which often plan such voyages. Members, of course, get a discount, but nonmembers are usually able to book passage, especially if the group has space available and is anxious to sell out their inventory of cabins.

Even without special themes, cruise liners normally offer a diverse range of shipboard activities featuring wine tastings, cooking demonstrations, fitness classes, and even elementary language instruction. All of this, of course, is in addition to the usual sports and recreation facilities.

TYPES OF CABINS AND STATEROOMS

Since your cabin will be your home at sea for a period of time, selection is of paramount importance. Your individual budget will determine the type of accommodations, i.e., size, deck level, and location (inside or outside cabin). Ambiance and amenities will vary greatly from one ship to another.

If you happen to live within driving distance of the home port of the vessel you are considering, a personal inspection is your best bet. You can usually arrange in advance to look at cabins and other facilities while passengers are boarding. Check the size of beds and bathroom facilities. The former can often be narrow bench-type cots, and the latter require a shoehorn to get into.

Charts, plans, and pictures in brochures tend to glamorize the situation and distort sizes. Some of the amenities found on board the newer liners include air conditioning, room telephones, radio, television, and, in some cases, VCRs. While these items are not of paramount importance (remember your cabin is for sleeping), these touches of luxury add considerably to the ambiance of the trip.

DINING AT SEA

Under the "uniclass" system, most ships have one main dining salon and usually provide two seatings at each meal. You can book your seating at the time you make your reservation or when you board the vessel. A special desk is available for this purpose. If you like to linger over your meal, book the second seating. On the other hand, if you get hungry early, opt for the first seating. You can also request a table for two or, if you prefer, join another couple or a larger group.

The chances of your getting hungry are slim, since food service at sea is truly a "movable feast." Most ships offer morning and afternoon teas and buffets, midnight suppers, and have snack shop facilities. The gourmand can consume six meals a day. With the exception of alcoholic beverages or special wines served with meals, you can eat to your heart's content without additional charge. Since the ship is your hotel, food service continues even when visiting a port.

While galleys try to provide a large selection of dishes and food styles, the basic cooking repertoire will usually reflect the nationality of the vessel. So, if you're not crazy about Greek food, you should think twice before booking a vessel that features that cuisine.

The quality of food and service is a major element of your cruise, and the best sources of information are the personal experience of friends or travel agents who have sailed on the vessel. Remember, all of your meals will be coming from one source, and the food can make or break your trip. Since crew members serve long periods at sea, try to ascertain if the chef and his staff will be just starting out on their term or ending many months at sea, looking forward to furlough. It can make a difference.

DUTY-FREE SHOPPING

Many ships have duty-free stores that offer merchandise similar to goods found at shops ashore. It pays to do some comparative pricing before deciding on any purchases. It is the policy of many operators to hold special sales on duty-free items after the ship has sailed from its last port of call.

DRESS AND SPECIAL EVENTS

The need to "dress" for dinner each evening at sea ended some years ago, and it is one of the reasons cruising has gained in popularity. Almost every cruise of at least a week's duration features a captain's reception or dinner the evening of the first full day at sea.

While many passengers don formal wear for the evening's festivities, suits for men and cocktail dresses for ladies are most acceptable. Let good taste be your guide. Remember, you will be meeting the captain and his staff, and the ship's photographer will be lurking nearby.

Generally, you will find that the longer the cruise, the more "dress" events may be scheduled. You will also want to check the itinerary for special shipboard galas with set themes calling for appropriate costumes. Once again, this is optional.

TIPPING

Even though some shipping companies have experimented with "no tipping" policies, tipping is still necessary on most voyages. In some cases you will be advised to tip in bulk in specified amounts. The money is then divided among the various service crew members.

The cabin steward and stewardess and the dining room steward directly affect your welfare at sea and should be tipped accordingly. Follow the advice of your tour material, or figure about $3.00 per person per day for each. Some ships suggest a percentage of your cabin rate, divided according to a supplied schedule. Often envelopes will be provided for tipping.

The rest is up to you and a matter of personal experience. If you regularly order wine at dinner, tip the wine steward a dollar a bottle or 10 percent of the total. The wine steward's gratuity may be added to your running wine tab. If the barman in the Crow's Nest Salon always remembered to stir, not shake, your evening martini, or the hairdresser did an extra special job preparing you for carnival night, tip accordingly.

LANGUAGE OF THE SEA

Lest you be mistaken for a "landlubber" try to pepper your conversation with the following key words:

CRUISE PLANNING

AFT:	The general direction from wherever you are to the rear of the vessel.
BERTH:	Where you and the boat rest.
BOW:	The front of the ship.
BRIDGE:	The Captain's domain atop the passenger section of the ship. It is the control room of the ship, and under certain conditions an appointment can be made for a visit.
BULKHEAD:	Any wall or partition.
DECK:	Any floor or level on a ship.
FORWARD:	The general direction from wherever you are to the front of the vessel.
MIDSHIPS:	The center of the boat.
OVERHEAD:	The ceiling.
PORT:	The left-hand side of the vessel.
POSH:	"Port Outbound, Starboard Home." The best accommodations, on the shady, cooler side of the boat back in the days when Britannia ruled the waves and there was steady traffic between the British Isles and ports east of Suez.
QUAY:	The word for a pier or dock in certain countries.
ST. ELMO'S FIRE:	St. Elmo is the patron saint of sailors and his "fire," caused by static electricity, can be seen at night atop the waves.

CRUISE PLANNING

STARBOARD: The right-hand side of the vessel.

STERN: The rear of the vessel.

WEATHER-DECK: A deck exposed to the elements.

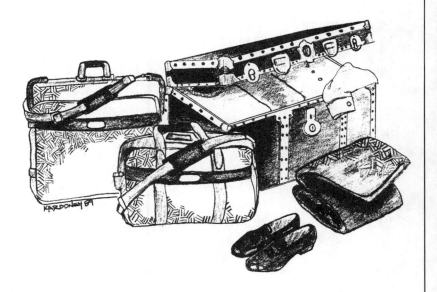

1990

S	M	T	W	T	F	S
JANUARY						
	1	2	3	4	5	6
7	8	9	10	11	12	13
14	15	16	17	18	19	20
21	22	23	24	25	26	27
28	29	30	31			

S	M	T	W	T	F	S
MAY						
		1	2	3	4	5
6	7	8	9	10	11	12
13	14	15	16	17	18	19
20	21	22	23	24	25	26
27	28	29	30	31		

S	M	T	W	T	F	S
SEPTEMBER						
						1
2	3	4	5	6	7	8
9	10	11	12	13	14	15
16	17	18	19	20	21	22
23	24	25	26	27	28	29
30						

S	M	T	W	T	F	S
FEBRUARY						
				1	2	3
4	5	6	7	8	9	10
11	12	13	14	15	16	17
18	19	20	21	22	23	24
25	26	27	28			

S	M	T	W	T	F	S
JUNE						
					1	2
3	4	5	6	7	8	9
10	11	12	13	14	15	16
17	18	19	20	21	22	23
24	25	26	27	28	29	30

S	M	T	W	T	F	S
OCTOBER						
	1	2	3	4	5	6
7	8	9	10	11	12	13
14	15	16	17	18	19	20
21	22	23	24	25	26	27
28	29	30	31			

S	M	T	W	T	F	S
MARCH						
				1	2	3
4	5	6	7	8	9	10
11	12	13	14	15	16	17
18	19	20	21	22	23	24
25	26	27	28	29	30	31

S	M	T	W	T	F	S
JULY						
1	2	3	4	5	6	7
8	9	10	11	12	13	14
15	16	17	18	19	20	21
22	23	24	25	26	27	28
29	30	31				

S	M	T	W	T	F	S
NOVEMBER						
				1	2	3
4	5	6	7	8	9	10
11	12	13	14	15	16	17
18	19	20	21	22	23	24
25	26	27	28	29	30	

S	M	T	W	T	F	S
APRIL						
1	2	3	4	5	6	7
8	9	10	11	12	13	14
15	16	17	18	19	20	21
22	23	24	25	26	27	28
29	30					

S	M	T	W	T	F	S
AUGUST						
			1	2	3	4
5	6	7	8	9	10	11
12	13	14	15	16	17	18
19	20	21	22	23	24	25
26	27	28	29	30	31	

S	M	T	W	T	F	S
DECEMBER						
						1
2	3	4	5	6	7	8
9	10	11	12	13	14	15
16	17	18	19	20	21	22
23	24	25	26	27	28	29
30	31					

1991

JANUARY
S	M	T	W	T	F	S
		1	2	3	4	5
6	7	8	9	10	11	12
13	14	15	16	17	18	19
20	21	22	23	24	25	26
27	28	29	30	31		

JULY
S	M	T	W	T	F	S
	1	2	3	4	5	6
7	8	9	10	11	12	13
14	15	16	17	18	19	20
21	22	23	24	25	26	27
28	29	30	31			

FEBRUARY
S	M	T	W	T	F	S
					1	2
3	4	5	6	7	8	9
10	11	12	13	14	15	16
17	18	19	20	21	22	23
24	25	26	27	28		

AUGUST
S	M	T	W	T	F	S
				1	2	3
4	5	6	7	8	9	10
11	12	13	14	15	16	17
18	19	20	21	22	23	24
25	26	27	28	29	30	31

MARCH
S	M	T	W	T	F	S
					1	2
3	4	5	6	7	8	9
10	11	12	13	14	15	16
17	18	19	20	21	22	23
24	25	26	27	28	29	30
31						

SEPTEMBER
S	M	T	W	T	F	S
1	2	3	4	5	6	7
8	9	10	11	12	13	14
15	16	17	18	19	20	21
22	23	24	25	26	27	28
29	30					

APRIL
S	M	T	W	T	F	S
	1	2	3	4	5	6
7	8	9	10	11	12	13
14	15	16	17	18	19	20
21	22	23	24	25	26	27
28	29	30				

OCTOBER
S	M	T	W	T	F	S
		1	2	3	4	5
6	7	8	9	10	11	12
13	14	15	16	17	18	19
20	21	22	23	24	25	26
27	28	29	30	31		

MAY
S	M	T	W	T	F	S
			1	2	3	4
5	6	7	8	9	10	11
12	13	14	15	16	17	18
19	20	21	22	23	24	25
26	27	28	29	30	31	

NOVEMBER
S	M	T	W	T	F	S
					1	2
3	4	5	6	7	8	9
10	11	12	13	14	15	16
17	18	19	20	21	22	23
24	25	26	27	28	29	30

JUNE
S	M	T	W	T	F	S
						1
2	3	4	5	6	7	8
9	10	11	12	13	14	15
16	17	18	19	20	21	22
23	24	25	26	27	28	29
30						

DECEMBER
S	M	T	W	T	F	S
1	2	3	4	5	6	7
8	9	10	11	12	13	14
15	16	17	18	19	20	21
22	23	24	25	26	27	28
29	30	31				

1992

JANUARY
S	M	T	W	T	F	S
			1	2	3	4
5	6	7	8	9	10	11
12	13	14	15	16	17	18
19	20	21	22	23	24	25
26	27	28	29	30	31	

JULY
S	M	T	W	T	F	S
			1	2	3	4
5	6	7	8	9	10	11
12	13	14	15	16	17	18
19	20	21	22	23	24	25
26	27	28	29	30	31	

FEBRUARY
S	M	T	W	T	F	S
						1
2	3	4	5	6	7	8
9	10	11	12	13	14	15
16	17	18	19	20	21	22
23	24	25	26	27	28	29

AUGUST
S	M	T	W	T	F	S
						1
2	3	4	5	6	7	8
9	10	11	12	13	14	15
16	17	18	19	20	21	22
23	24	25	26	27	28	29
30	31					

MARCH
S	M	T	W	T	F	S
1	2	3	4	5	6	7
8	9	10	11	12	13	14
15	16	17	18	19	20	21
22	23	24	25	26	27	28
29	30	31				

SEPTEMBER
S	M	T	W	T	F	S
		1	2	3	4	5
6	7	8	9	10	11	12
13	14	15	16	17	18	19
20	21	22	23	24	25	26
27	28	29	30			

APRIL
S	M	T	W	T	F	S
			1	2	3	4
5	6	7	8	9	10	11
12	13	14	15	16	17	18
19	20	21	22	23	24	25
26	27	28	29	30		

OCTOBER
S	M	T	W	T	F	S
				1	2	3
4	5	6	7	8	9	10
11	12	13	14	15	16	17
18	19	20	21	22	23	24
25	26	27	28	29	30	31

MAY
S	M	T	W	T	F	S
					1	2
3	4	5	6	7	8	9
10	11	12	13	14	15	16
17	18	19	20	21	22	23
24	25	26	27	28	29	30
31						

NOVEMBER
S	M	T	W	T	F	S
1	2	3	4	5	6	7
8	9	10	11	12	13	14
15	16	17	18	19	20	21
22	23	24	25	26	27	28
29	30					

JUNE
S	M	T	W	T	F	S
	1	2	3	4	5	6
7	8	9	10	11	12	13
14	15	16	17	18	19	20
21	22	23	24	25	26	27
28	29	30				

DECEMBER
S	M	T	W	T	F	S
		1	2	3	4	5
6	7	8	9	10	11	12
13	14	15	16	17	18	19
20	21	22	23	24	25	26
27	28	29	30	31		

U.S. HOLIDAYS

HOLIDAY	1990	1991	1992
New Year's Day	Mon./Jan. 1	Tue./Jan. 1	Wed./Jan. 1
Martin Luther King's Birthday (Observed)	Mon./Jan. 15	Mon./Jan. 21	Mon./Jan. 20
Ash Wednesday	Wed./Feb. 28	Wed./Feb. 13	Wed./Mar. 4
Valentine's Day	Wed./Feb. 14	Thu./Feb. 14	Fri./Feb. 14
Presidents' Day	Mon./Feb. 19	Mon./Feb. 18	Mon./Feb. 17
St. Patrick's Day	Sat./Mar. 17	Sun./Mar. 17	Tue./Mar. 17
Palm Sunday	Sun./Apr. 8	Sun./Mar. 24	Sun./Apr. 12
Passover	Tue./Apr. 10	Sat./Mar. 30	Sat./Apr. 18
Good Friday	Fri./Apr. 13	Fri./Mar. 29	Fri./Apr. 17
Easter Sunday	Sun./Apr. 15	Sun./Mar. 31	Sun./Apr. 19
Mother's Day	Sun./May 13	Sun./May 12	Sun./May 10
Armed Forces Day	Sat./May 19	Sat./May 18	Sat./May 16
Memorial Day	Mon./May 28	Mon./May 27	Mon./May 25
Flag Day	Thu./Jun. 14	Fri./Jun. 14	Sun./Jun. 14
Father's Day	Sun./Jun. 17	Sun./Jun. 16	Sun./Jun. 21
Independence Day	Wed./Jul. 4	Thur./Jul. 4	Sat./Jul. 4
Labor Day	Mon./Sep. 3	Mon./Sep. 2	Mon./ Sep. 7
Rosh Hashanah	Thu./Sep. 20	Mon./Sep. 9	Mon./ Sep. 28
Yom Kippur	Sat./Sep. 29	Wed./Sep. 18	Wed./Oct. 7
Columbus Day (Observed)	Mon./Oct. 8	Mon./Oct. 14	Mon./Oct. 12
Halloween	Wed./Oct. 31	Thu./Oct. 31	Sat./Oct. 31
Election Day	Tue./Nov. 6	Tue./Nov. 5	Tue./Nov. 3
Veterans Day	Sun./Nov. 11	Mon./Nov. 11	Wed./Nov. 11
Thanksgiving Day	Thu./Nov. 22	Thu./Nov. 28	Thu. Nov. 26
Hanukkah	Wed./Dec. 12	Mon./Dec. 2	Sun./Dec. 20
Christmas Day	Tue./Dec. 25	Wed./Dec. 25	Fri./Dec. 25

INTERNATIONAL HOLIDAYS

Many holidays are linked to the lunar calendar and are not fixed on a particular date. The dates of Jewish and many Christian holidays vary from year to year as does the month of Ramadan which is observed throughout the Muslim world. It is best to check with a travel agent or tourist board before leaving. January 1, May 1, Good Friday, Easter Sunday and Christmas Day are observed in most countries in the world.

ARGENTINA	May 25, June 20, July 9, August 17, October 12
AUSTRALIA	January 26, April 25, December 26
BELGIUM	July 21, August 15, November 1, November 11
BRAZIL	Carnival (3 days preceding Lent), April 21, September 7, November 2, November 15
CANADA	July 1, November 11, December 26
CHINA	Spring Festival—Lunar New Year (3 days), October 1, 2
FRANCE	May 8, July 14, August 15, November 1, November 11
GERMANY (WEST)	January 6, June 17, August 15, November 1, December 26
GREECE	January 6, March 25, August 15, October 28, December 26
INDIA	January 26, August 15, October 2

INTERNATIONAL HOLIDAYS

ISRAEL

All variable dates. No business transacted Saturdays.

ITALY

January 6, April 25, August 15, November 1, December 8, December 26

JAPAN

January 15, February 11, April 29, May 3, September 15, October 10, November 3, 23, New Year Holiday begins on December 28. The vernal and autumnal equinoxes are also observed as holidays.

MEXICO

January 6, February 5, February 24, March 21, May 5, August 15, September 1, 16, October 12, November 1, 2, 20, December 12

SPAIN

January 6, March 19, June 21, July 25, August 15, October 12, November 18, December 8

UK

Bank Holidays vary, December 26

USSR

March 8, May 1-2, May 9, October 7, November 7-8

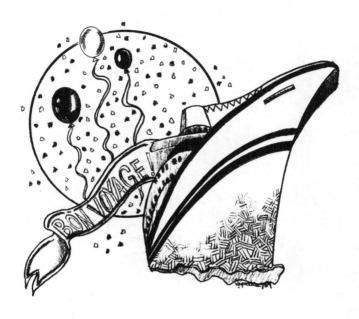

"*But O the ship, the immortal ship! O ship aboard the ship!*
Ship of the body, ship of the soul, voyaging, voyaging, voyaging."

Walt Whitman

CHECKLIST

THINGS TO DO BEFORE LEAVING

_____ Check expiration dates on passports and credit cards

_____ Secure necessary visas

_____ Check with doctor and dentist

_____ Arrange for mail to be held and newspapers to be picked up

_____ Purchase small amount of foreign currency for each destination for immediate expenses

_____ Purchase traveler's checks

_____ Arrange for care of pets and plants

_____ Pay necessary bills

_____ Check on water and electricity

_____ Leave a copy of your itinerary with a friend or neighbor

_____ Tag all luggage on the outside and include an i.d. tag inside.

_____ Purchase extra film and batteries

_____ Set burglar alarms or take other security measures

AND DON'T FORGET TO TAKE:

_____ Passport

_____ Visas

_____ Tickets

_____ Credit cards

_____ Traveler's checks

_____ Prescriptions/Medications

PACKING LIST

LADIES

_____ Accessories (jewelry, scarves, etc.)

_____ Bathing suit

_____ Beach robe

_____ Blouses

_____ Dresses

_____ Dressing gown (robe)

_____ Hair conditioner

_____ Hair curlers

_____ Hair dryer

_____ Shampoo

_____ Makeup

_____ Mirror (folding)

_____ Nightgown

_____ Raincoat/Boots (light, folding)

_____ _____

_____ _____

_____ _____

_____ _____

_____ _____

_____ _____

_____ Razor/blades

_____ Shoes (dress, walking, exercise)

_____ Skirts

_____ Slacks

_____ Slippers

_____ Slips

_____ Sportswear/Equipment

_____ Stockings/Socks

_____ Suit

_____ Sweaters

_____ Toothbrush/toothpaste

_____ Underwear

_____ _____

_____ _____

_____ _____

_____ _____

_____ _____

_____ _____

PACKING LIST

GENTLEMEN

_____ Accessories (cuff links, tie clasps, jewelry, etc.)

_____ Bathing suit

_____ Beach robe

_____ Belts/Braces (suspenders)

_____ Dressing gown (robe)

_____ Hair conditioner

_____ Hair dryer

_____ Shampoo

_____ Handkerchiefs

_____ Pajamas

_____ Raincoat (light, folding)

_____ Razor/blades/ shaving cream

_____ Shirts

_____ Shoes/Socks

_____ Slacks

_____ Slippers

_____ Sportswear/ Equipment

_____ Sport coat

_____ Suits

_____ Sunscreen lotion

_____ Ties

_____ Toothbrush/ toothpaste

_____ Underwear

_____ _____

_____ _____

_____ _____

_____ _____

_____ _____

_____ _____

_____ _____

_____ _____

_____ _____

_____ _____

_____ _____

_____ _____

_____ _____

_____ _____

_____ _____

_____ _____

CHECKLIST

GENERAL PACKING LIST

_____ Books (Tour guide, Map)

_____ Calculator (pocket size)

_____ Camera/Film/Batteries

_____ Driver's license

_____ Empty shopping bag

_____ Flashlight (pocket size)

_____ Glasses (prescription eyeglasses and sunglasses)

_____ Itinerary

_____ Language/Phrase book

_____ Medicine (prescription drugs, anti-diarrhea pills, digestive aids)

_____ Micro-cassette recorder

_____ Passport/Visa (if needed)

_____ Radio (transistor)

_____ Slippers for in-flight comfort

_____ Sunscreen lotion

_____ Tissues

_____ Tickets (airline, ship, train, etc.)

_____ Umbrella (small, folding)

_____ Voltage converter(s)

_____ _____

_____ _____

_____ _____

_____ _____

ITINERARY

Travel Agent _____ Telephone _____

Address _____

_____

Notes _____

_____

_____

_____

_____

_____

Departing from _____

Date _____

Traveling by _____

Reservation/Flight # _____

Arriving at _____

Date _____

Car Rental/Confirmation # _____

Departing from _____

Date _____

Traveling by _____

Reservation/Flight # _____

Arriving at _____

Date _____

Car Rental/Confirmation # _____

ITINERARY

Departing from _____

Date _____

Traveling by _____

Reservation/Flight # _____

Arriving at _____

Date _____

Car Rental/Confirmation # _____

Departing from _____

Date _____

Traveling by _____

Reservation/Flight # _____

Arriving at _____

Date _____

Car Rental/Confirmation # _____

Departing from _____

Date _____

Traveling by _____

Reservation/Flight # _____

Arriving at _____

Date _____

Car Rental/Confirmation # _____

ITINERARY

Departing from _____

Date _____

Traveling by _____

Reservation/Flight # _____

Arriving at _____

Date _____

Car Rental/Confirmation # _____

Departing from _____

Date _____

Traveling by _____

Reservation/Flight # _____

Arriving at _____

Date _____

Car Rental/Confirmation # _____

*"For my part, I travel not to go anywhere, but to go. I travel
for travel's sake."*

Robert Louis Stevenson

HOTELS

City _____

Name of Hotel _____ Telephone _____

Address _____

Confirmation # _____

Contacts _____

Remarks _____

_____

City _____

Name of Hotel _____ Telephone _____

Address _____

Confirmation # _____

Contacts _____

Remarks _____

_____

City _____

Name of Hotel _____ Telephone _____

Address _____

Confirmation # _____

Contacts _____

Remarks _____

_____

HOTELS

City _____

Name of Hotel _____ Telephone _____

Address _____

Confirmation # _____

Contacts _____

Remarks _____

_____

City _____

Name of Hotel _____ Telephone _____

Address _____

Confirmation # _____

Contacts _____

Remarks _____

_____

"All saints can do miracles, but few of them can keep hotels."
Mark Twain

HOTELS

City _____

Name of Hotel _____ Telephone _____

Address _____

Confirmation # _____

Contacts _____

Remarks _____

_____

City _____

Name of Hotel _____ Telephone _____

Address _____

Confirmation # _____

Contacts _____

Remarks _____

_____

City _____

Name of Hotel _____ Telephone _____

Address _____

Confirmation # _____

Contacts _____

Remarks _____

_____

HOTELS

City _____

Name of Hotel _____ Telephone _____

Address _____

Confirmation # _____

Contacts _____

Remarks _____

_____

City _____

Name of Hotel _____ Telephone _____

Address _____

Confirmation # _____

Contacts _____

Remarks _____

_____

City _____

Name of Hotel _____ Telephone _____

Address _____

Confirmation # _____

Contacts _____

Remarks _____

_____

THINGS TO SEE

Museums _____

_____

_____

_____

_____

_____

_____

_____

Churches _____

_____

_____

_____

_____

_____

_____

_____

Sights of Interest _____

_____

_____

_____

_____

_____

_____

_____

Excursions _____

_____

_____

_____

_____

_____

_____

_____

THINGS TO SEE

Museums _____
_____
_____
_____
_____
_____
_____
_____
_____

Churches _____
_____
_____
_____
_____
_____
_____
_____
_____

Sights of Interest _____
_____
_____
_____
_____
_____
_____
_____
_____

"Welcome is the best cheer."

Thomas Fuller

WEEK BY WEEK

Monday _____

_____

_____

_____

_____

_____

_____

_____

Tuesday _____

_____

_____

_____

_____

_____

_____

_____

Wednesday _____

_____

_____

_____

_____

_____

_____

_____

Thursday _____

_____

_____

_____

_____

_____

_____

_____

Friday _____

_____

_____

_____

_____

_____

_____

_____

Saturday _____

_____

_____

_____

_____

_____

_____

_____

Sunday _____

_____

_____

_____

_____

_____

_____

_____

"The heaviest baggage for a traveler is an empty purse."
English proverb

WEEK BY WEEK

Monday _____

_____
_____
_____
_____
_____
_____
_____

Tuesday _____

_____
_____
_____
_____
_____
_____
_____

Wednesday _____

_____
_____
_____
_____
_____
_____
_____

Thursday _____

_____
_____
_____
_____
_____
_____
_____

Friday _____

_____
_____
_____
_____
_____
_____
_____

Saturday _____

_____
_____
_____
_____
_____
_____
_____

Sunday _____

_____
_____
_____
_____
_____
_____

"Happy he who like Ulysses has made a glorious voyage."
Joachim du Bellay

WEEK BY WEEK

Monday _____

_____

_____

_____

_____

_____

_____

_____

Tuesday _____

_____

_____

_____

_____

_____

_____

_____

Wednesday _____

_____

_____

_____

_____

_____

_____

_____

Thursday _____

_____

_____

_____

_____

_____

_____

_____

WEEK BY WEEK

Friday ————————————————————

Saturday ————————————————————

Sunday ————————————————————

"The journey not the arrival matters."
Montaigne

KAROONEY '89

WEEK BY WEEK

Monday _____
_____
_____
_____
_____
_____
_____
_____

Tuesday _____
_____
_____
_____
_____
_____
_____
_____

Wednesday _____
_____
_____
_____
_____
_____
_____
_____

Thursday _____
_____
_____
_____
_____
_____
_____
_____

Friday _____

_____

_____

_____

_____

_____

_____

_____

Saturday _____

_____

_____

_____

_____

_____

_____

_____

Sunday _____

_____

_____

_____

_____

_____

_____

"One travels more usefully when alone, because he reflects more."

Thomas Jefferson

WEEK BY WEEK

Monday _____

_____

_____

_____

_____

_____

_____

Tuesday _____

_____

_____

_____

_____

_____

_____

Wednesday _____

_____

_____

_____

_____

_____

_____

Thursday _____

_____

_____

_____

_____

_____

_____

Friday _____

_____
_____
_____
_____
_____
_____
_____
_____
_____

Saturday _____

_____
_____
_____
_____
_____
_____
_____
_____
_____

Sunday _____

_____
_____
_____
_____
_____
_____
_____
_____

"Ay, now am I in Arden; the more fool I: when I was at home, I was in a better place but travelers must be content."
William Shakespeare

WEEK BY WEEK

Monday _____

_____

_____

_____

_____

_____

_____

_____

Tuesday _____

_____

_____

_____

_____

_____

_____

_____

Wednesday _____

_____

_____

_____

_____

_____

_____

_____

Thursday _____

_____

_____

_____

_____

_____

_____

_____

Friday _____

_____

_____

_____

_____

_____

_____

_____

Saturday _____

_____

_____

_____

_____

_____

_____

Sunday _____

_____

_____

_____

_____

_____

"Life is either a daring adventure or nothing."

Helen Keller

EXPENSES

Date	Item	Amount Foreign	Amount Dollars

EXPENSES

Date	Item	Amount Foreign	Amount Dollars

EXPENSES

Date	Item	Amount Foreign	Amount Dollars

EXPENSES

Date	Item	Amount Foreign	Amount Dollars

READING LIST

"To read a writer is for me not merely to get an idea of what he says, but to go off with him, and travel in his company."
André Gide

PHOTOS

Paste in photo highlights of your trip here.

PHOTOS

PHOTOS

RECIPES

_____

_____
_____
_____
_____
_____
_____
_____

_____   _____
_____   _____
_____   _____
_____   _____
_____   _____
_____   _____
_____   _____

"A man seldom thinks with more earnestness of anything than he does of his dinner."

Samuel Johnson

RECIPES

_____

_____
_____
_____
_____
_____
_____
_____
_____
_____
_____
_____
_____
_____
_____

"The discovery of a new dish does more for the happiness of mankind than the discovery of a star."

Brillat-Savarin

"I never travel without my diary. One should always have something sensational to read on the train."

Oscar Wilde

DIARY

DIARY

DIARY

DIARY

DIARY

DIARY

DIARY

DIARY

DIARY

DIARY

DIARY

DIARY

DIARY

DIARY

DIARY

DIARY

DIARY

DIARY

DIARY

DIARY

DIARY

DIARY

DIARY

DIARY

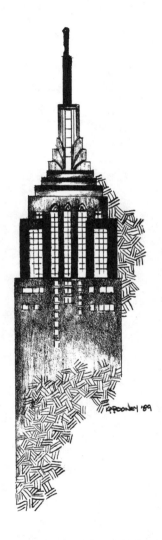

"*In traveling, a man must carry knowledge with him if he would bring home knowledge.*"

Samuel Johnson

U.S. AREA CODES

ALABAMA	
All phones	205
ALASKA	
All phones	907
ARIZONA	
All phones	602
ARKANSAS	
All phones	501
CALIFORNIA	
Alameda	415
Alhambra	818
Anaheim	714
Bakersfield	805
Baldwin Park	818
Bellflower	213
Berkeley	415
Beverly Hills	213
Buena Park	714
Burbank	818
Carson	213
Chula Vista	619
Compton	213
Concord	415
Costa Mesa	714
Covina	213
Culver City	213
Daly City	415
Davis	916
Downey	213
El Monte	818
Escondido	619
Eureka	707
Fairfield	707
Fountain Valley	714
Fremont	415
Fresno	209
Fullerton	714
Gardena	213
Garden Grove	714
Glendale	818
Hacienda Heights	818
Hawthorne	213
Hollywood	213
Huntington Beach	714
Huntington Park	213
Inglewood	213
Lakewood	213
La Mesa	619
Livermore	415
Lodi	209
Long Beach	213
Los Angeles	213
Lynwood	213
Manhattan Beach	213
Menlo Park	415
Modesto	209
Montebello	213
Monterey	408
Monterey Park	818
Napa	707
National City	619
Newport Beach	714
Norwalk	213
Novato	415
Oakland	415
Oceanside	619
Ontario	714
Orange	714
Oxnard	805
Palo Alto	415
Pasadena	818
Redlands	714
Redondo Beach	213
Redwood City	415
Richmond	415
Riverside	714
Sacramento	916
Salinas	408
San Bernardino	714
San Bruno	415
San Diego	619
San Francisco	415
San Jose	408
San Leandro	415
San Luis Obispo	805
Santa Ana	714
Santa Barbara	805
Santa Clara	408
Santa Cruz	408
Santa Monica	213
Santa Rosa	707
Simi Valley	805
South Gate	213
South San Francisco	415
Stockton	209
Sunnyvale	408
Thousand Oaks	805
Torrance	213
Vallejo	707
Ventura	805
Walnut Creek	415
West Covina	818
West Hollywood	213
Westminster	714
Whittier	213
COLORADO	
Aspen	303
Colorado Springs	719
Denver	303
Pueblo	719
Vail	303
CONNECTICUT	
All phones	203
DELAWARE	
All phones	302
FLORIDA	
Boca Raton	407
Clearwater	813
Coral Gables	305
Daytona Beach	904
Fort Lauderdale	305
Fort Myers	813
Gainesville	904
Hialeah	305
Jacksonville	904
Kendall	305
Key West	305
Lakeland	813
Melbourne	407
Miami	305
Miami Beach	305
Miramar	305
North Miami	305
North Miami Beach	305
Orlando	407
Pensacola	904
Plantation	305
Pompano Beach	305
St. Petersburg	813
Sarasota	813
Tallahassee	904
Tampa	813
West Palm Beach	407
GEORGIA	
Albany	912
Athens	404
Atlanta	404
Augusta	404
Columbus	404
Fort Benning	404
Gainesville	404
Macon	912
Rome	404
Savannah	912
HAWAII	
All phones	808
IDAHO	
All phones	208
ILLINOIS	
Arlington Heights	312
Aurora	312
Berwyn	312
Bloomington	309
Carbondale	618
Champaign-Urbana	217
Chicago	312
Cicero	312
Decatur	217
De Kalb	815
Des Plaines	312
East St. Louis	618
Elgin	312
Evanston	312
Harvey	312
Joliet	815
Melrose Park	312
Moline	309
Mount Prospect	312
Naperville	312
Oak Lawn	312
Oak Park	312
Peoria	309
Rockford	815
Rock Island	309
Schaumburg	312
Skokie	312
Springfield	217
Waukegan	312
Wheaton	312
Wilmette	312
INDIANA	
Anderson	317
Bloomington	812
Elkhart	219
Evansville	812
Fort Wayne	219
Gary	219
Hammond	219
Indianapolis	317
Kokomo	317
Lafayette	317
Mishawaka	219
Muncie	317
Richmond	317
South Bend	219
Terre Haute	812
IOWA	
Ames	515
Cedar Rapids	319
Council Bluffs	712
Davenport	319
Des Moines	515
Dubuque	319
Iowa City	319
Sioux City	712
Waterloo	319
KANSAS	
Hutchinson	316
Kansas City	913
Lawrence	913
Overland Park	913
Salina	913
Topeka	913
Wichita	316
KENTUCKY	
Bowling Green	502
Covington	606
Lexington	606
Louisville	502
Owensboro	502
LOUISIANA	
Alexandria	318
Baton Rouge	504
Bossier City	318
Kenner	504
Lafayette	318
Lake Charles	318
Marrero	504
Metairie	504
Monroe	318
New Orleans	504
Shreveport	318
MAINE	
All phones	207
MARYLAND	
All phones	301
MASSACHUSETTS	
Arlington	617
Boston	617
Brockton	617
Brookline	617
Cambridge	617
Chicopee	413
Everett	617
Fall River	508
Fitchburg	508
Framingham	508
Haverhill	508
Holyoke	413
Lawrence	508
Lexington	617
Lowell	508
Lynn	617
Malden	617
Medford	617
New Bedford	508
Newton	617
Peabody	617
Pittsfield	413
Quincy	617
Reading	617
Revere	617
Roxbury	617
Salem	617
Somerville	617
Springfield	413
Taunton	508
Waltham	617
Wellesley	617
West Springfield	413
Weymouth	617
Worcester	617
MICHIGAN	
Ann Arbor	313
Battle Creek	616
Bay City	517
Dearborn	313
Detroit	313
East Detroit	313
East Lansing	517
Flint	313
Grand Rapids	616
Jackson	517
Kalamazoo	616
Lansing	517
Livonia	313
Marquette	906
Muskegon	616
Pontiac	313
Roseville	313
Royal Oak	313
Saginaw	517
St. Clair Shores	313
Southfield	313
Sterling Heights	313
Taylor	313
Troy	313
Warren	313
Westland	313
Wyoming	616
MINNESOTA	
Bloomington	612
Duluth	218
Edina	612
Minneapolis	612
Minnetonka	612
Rochester	507
St. Cloud	612
St. Louis Park	612
St. Paul	612
MISSISSIPPI	
All phones	601
MISSOURI	
Columbia	314
Florissant	314
Fort Leonard Wood	314
Independence	816
Joplin	417
Kansas City	816
St. Charles	314
St. Joseph	816
St. Louis	314
Springfield	417
University City	314
MONTANA	
All phones	406
NEBRASKA	
Hastings	402
Lincoln	402
Omaha	402
NEVADA	
All phones	702
NEW HAMPSHIRE	
All phones	603
NEW JERSEY	
Asbury Park	201
Atlantic City	609
Bayonne	201
Bellmawr	609
Burlington	609
Camden	609
Clifton	201
East Orange	201
Eatontown	201
Elizabeth	201
Englewood	201
Fair Lawn	201
Fort Dix	609
Fort Lee	201
Hackensack	201
Hoboken	201
Jersey City	201
Kearny	201
Lakewood	201
Linden	201
Long Beach	609
Madison	201
Metuchen	201
Middlesex	201
Millburn	201
Montclair	201
Morristown	201
Newark	201
New Brunswick	201
North Plainfield	201
Nutley	201

U.S. AREA CODES

City	Code	City	Code	City	Code
Orange	201	Larchmont	914	Woodmere	516
Paramus	201	Levittown	516	Woodstock	914
Passaic	201	Lindenhurst	516	Wyandanch	516
Paterson	201	Lockport	716	Yonkers	914
Perth Amboy	201	Long Beach	516	Yorktown Heights	914
Plainfield	201	Long Island	516		
Pleasantville	609	Lynbrook	516	**NORTH CAROLINA**	
Princeton	609	Mahopac	914	Asheville	704
Rahway	201	Mamaroneck	914	Chapel Hill	919
Red Bank	201	Manhasset	516	Charlotte	704
Ridgewood	201	Manhattan	212	Durham	919
Rutherford	201	Massapequa	516	Fayetteville	919
Sayreville	201	Middletown	914	Gastonia	704
Somerville	201	Mineola	516	Greenville	919
Summit	201	Montauk Point	516	High Point	919
Teaneck	201	Monticello	914	Raleigh	919
Trenton	609	Mount Kisco	914	Rocky Mount	919
Union City	201	Mount Vernon	914	Wilmington	919
Weehawken	201	Nanuet	914	Wilson	919
Westfield	201	Nassau County	516	Winston-Salem	919
West New York	201	Newburgh	914		
West Orange	201	New City	914	**NORTH DAKOTA**	
		New Rochelle	914	All phones	701
NEW MEXICO		New York City	212		
All phones	505	Niagara Falls	716	**OHIO**	
		Norwich	607	Akron	216
NEW YORK		Nyack	914	Canton	216
Albany	518	Oneonta	607	Cincinnati	513
Amagansett	516	Ossining	914	Cleveland	216
Amityville	516	Oswego	315	Columbus	614
Babylon	516	Pelham	914	Cuyahoga Falls	216
Bay Shore	516	Plattsburgh	518	Dayton	513
Bethpage	516	Pleasantville	914	East Cleveland	216
Binghamton	607	Port Chester	914	Elyria	216
Brewster	914	Port Jefferson	516	Euclid	216
Bridgehampton	516	Port Washington	516	Hamilton	513
Bronx	212	Potsdam	315	Kettering	513
Bronxville	914	Poughkeepsie	914	Lakewood	216
Brooklyn	718	Queens County	718	Lima	419
Buffalo	716	Riverhead	516	Lorain	216
Chappaqua	914	Rochester	716	Mansfield	419
Commack	516	Rockville Centre	516	Marion	614
Copiague	516	Rome	315	Mentor	216
Corning	607	Ronkonkoma	516	Middletown	513
Cortland	607	Roslyn	516	Newark	614
Croton-on-Hudson	914	Rye	914	Parma	216
Deer Park	516	Sag Harbor	516	Shaker Heights	216
Dobbs Ferry	914	Saratoga Springs	518	Springfield	513
Eastchester	914	Sayville	516	Toledo	419
East Hampton	516	Scarsdale	914	Warren	216
East Massapequa	516	Schenectady	518	Youngstown	216
East Meadow	516	Shelter Island	516		
Eastport	516	Sloatsburg	914	**OKLAHOMA**	
Ellenville	914	Smithtown	516	Enid	405
Elmira	607	Southampton	516	Lawton	405
Fallsburg	914	Spring Valley	914	Muskogee	918
Farmingdale	516	Staten Island	718	Oklahoma City	405
Fire Island	516	Stony Point	914	Stillwater	405
Fishers Island	516	Suffern	914	Tulsa	918
Floral Park	516	Suffolk County	516		
Freeport	516	Syracuse	315	**OREGON**	
Garden City	516	Tarrytown	914	All phones	503
Glen Cove	516	Ticonderoga	518		
Great Neck	516	Troy	518	**PENNSYLVANIA**	
Grossinger	914	Tuckahoe	914	Allentown	215
Hampton Bays	516	Uniondale	516	Altoona	814
Harrison	914	Utica	315	Bethlehem	215
Hastings-on-		Valley Stream	516	Chester	215
Hudson	914	Wantagh	516	Erie	814
Hicksville	516	Watertown	315	Harrisburg	717
Hudson	518	Westbury	516	Lancaster	717
Huntington	516	Westchester Co.	914	Levittown	215
Irvington	914	Westhampton	516	Philadelphia	215
Islip	516	West Hempstead	516	Pittsburgh	412
Ithaca	607	West Islip	516	Reading	215
Kingston	914	White Lake	914	Scranton	717
Lackawanna	716	White Plains	914	Wilkes-Barre	717
Lake Huntington	914	Williamsville	716	Wilkinsburg	412
Lake Success	516			York	717
				RHODE ISLAND	
				All phones	401

City	Code	City	Code
SOUTH CAROLINA		Everett	206
All phones	803	Richland	509
		Seattle	206
SOUTH DAKOTA		Spokane	509
All phones	605	Tacoma	206
		Vancouver	206
TENNESSEE		Yakima	509
Chattanooga	615		
Clarksville	615	**WEST VIRGINIA**	
Jackson	901	All phones	304
Johnson City	615		
Knoxville	615	**WISCONSIN**	
Memphis	901	Appleton	414
Nashville	615	Eau Claire	715
		Green Bay	414
TEXAS		Janesville	608
Abilene	915	Kenosha	414
Amarillo	806	La Crosse	608
Arlington	817	Madison	608
Austin	512	Milwaukee	414
Baytown	713	Oshkosh	414
Beaumont	409	Racine	414
Brownsville	512	Sheboygan	414
Bryan	409	Waukesha	414
Corpus Christi	512	Wauwatosa	414
Dallas	214	West Allis	414
Denton	817		
El Paso	915	**WYOMING**	
Fort Worth	817	All phones	307
Galveston	409		
Garland	214	**Outside the**	
Grand Prairie	214	**United States**	
Harlingen	512		
Houston	713		
Irving	214	**BERMUDA**	
Killeen	817	All phones	809
Laredo	512		
Longview	214	**CANADA**	
Lubbock	806		
McAllen	512	**ALBERTA**	
Mesquite	214	All phones	403
Midland	915		
Odessa	915	**BRITISH**	
Pasadena	713	**COLUMBIA**	
Port Arthur	409	All phones	604
Richardson	214		
San Angelo	915	**MANITOBA**	
San Antonio	512	All phones	204
Temple	817		
Tyler	214	**NEW BRUNSWICK**	
Victoria	512	All phones	506
Waco	817		
Wichita Falls	817	**NEWFOUNDLAND**	
		All phones	709
UTAH			
All phones	801	**NOVA SCOTIA**	
		All phones	902
VERMONT			
All phones	802	**ONTARIO**	
		Fort William	807
VIRGINIA		London	519
Alexandria	703	North Bay	705
Arlington	703	Ottawa	613
Charlottesville	804	Toronto	416
Chesapeake	804		
Danville	804	**QUEBEC**	
Hampton	804	Montreal	514
Lynchburg	804	Quebec	418
Newport News	804	Sherbrooke	819
Norfolk	804		
Petersburg	804	**SASKATCHEWAN**	
Portsmouth	804	All phones	306
Richmond	804		
Roanoke	703	**PUERTO RICO**	
Virginia Beach	804	All phones	809
WASHINGTON, D.C.		**VIRGIN ISLANDS**	
All phones	202	All phones	809
WASHINGTON STATE			
Bellevue	206		
Bellingham	206		

International Access Code + Country Code + City Code + Local Number
If your area has International Dialing, you can dial direct (without operator
assistance) to telephones in many parts of the world. First, dial 011, which
is the international access code. Immediately thereafter, dial the country
code (listed in boldface type) followed by the city code (listed in lightface
type) and then the local number (which you must obtain beforehand).

ANDORRA	**33**	Barranquilla	5	Frankfurt	69
All Points	628	Bogota	1	Hamburg	40
ARGENTINA	**54**	Bucaramanga	71	Munich	89
Buenos Aires	1	Cali	3	GREECE	**30**
Cordoba	51	COSTA RICA	**506**	Athens	1
La Plata	21	All points	*	Patrai	61
Rosario	41	CYPRUS	**357**	Thessaloniki	31
AUSTRALIA	**61**	Famagusta	31	Tripolis	71
Adelaide	8	Limassol	51	GUAM	**671**
Brisbane	7	Nicosia	21	All points	*
Melbourne	3	DENMARK	**45**	GUATEMALA	**502**
Sydney	2	Aalborg	8	Amatitlan	33
AUSTRIA	**43**	Aarhus	6	Antigua	9
Graz	316	Copenhagen	1 or 2	Guatemala City	2
Linz	732	Esbjerg	5	HAITI	**509**
Salzburg	6222	Odense	9	Cap Haitien	3
Vienna	1	ECUADOR	**593**	Gonaive	5
BAHRAIN	**973**	Cuenca	7	Port-au-Prince	1
All points	*	Guayaquil	4	HONDURAS	**504**
BELGIUM	**32**	Quito	2	All points	*
Antwerp	31	EL SALVADOR	**503**	HONG KONG	**852**
Bruges	50	All points	*	Castle Peak	12
Brussels	2	FIJI	**679**	Hong Kong	5
Ghent	91	All points	*	Lantau	5
Liege	41	FINLAND	**358**	Tsun Wan	12
BELIZE	**501**	Epoo-Ebbo	15	IRAN	**98**
Belize City	*	Helsinki	0	Esfahan	31
Belmopan	08	Tampere	31	Tabriz	41
Orange Walk	03	Turku-Abo	21	Teheran	21
BRAZIL	**55**	FRANCE	**33**	IRAQ	**964**
Belo Horizonte	31	Lyon	78	Baghdad	1
Porto Alegre	512	Marseille	91	IRELAND, REP. OF	**353**
Recife	81	Nice	93	Cork	21
Rio de Janeiro	21	Paris	13 or 14 or 16	Dublin	1
Salvador	71	Toulouse	61	Dundalk	42
Sao Paulo	11	GERMANY		Galway	91
CHILE	**56**	(EAST)	37	Waterford	51
Santiago	2	Berlin	2	ISRAEL	**972**
Valparaiso	31	Dresden	51	Bat Yam	3
Vina del Mar	31	Karl-Marx-Stadt	71	Haifa	4
CHINA (TAIWAN)	**886**	Leipzig	41	Jerusalem	2
Kaohsiung	7	GERMANY		Tel Aviv	3
Taichung	42	(WEST)	49	ITALY	**39**
Tainan	6	Berlin	30	Milan	2
Taipei	2	Dusseldorf	211	Naples	81
COLOMBIA	**57**	Essen	201	Rome	6

INTERNATIONAL DIALING

Turin	11	Oslo	2	Izmir	51	
JAPAN	81	Stavanger	45	UNITED ARAB		
Kobe	78	Trondheim	75	EMIRATES	1	
Kyoto	75	PAPUA		Abu Dhabi	2	
Nagoya	52	NEW GUINEA	675	Al Ain	3	
Osaka	6	All Points	*	Ajman	29	
Tokyo	3	PERU	51	All Points	29	
Yokohama	45	Arequipa	54	Dubai	978	
KENYA	254	Lima	14	Aweir	*	
Kisumu	35	Trujillo	44	Falaj Amala	96	
Mombasa	11	PHILIPPINES	63	Fujairah	1	
Nairobi	2	Cebu	32	All Points	1	
Nakuru	37	Davao	35	Ras-al-Khaimah	7	
KOREA	82	Manila	2	All Points	7	
Inchon	32	PORTUGAL	351	Sharjah	5	
Pusan	51	Coimbra	39	All Points	5	
Seoul	2	Lisbon	1	Umm-al-Quwain	69	
Taegu	82	SAN MARINO	39	All Points	69	
KUWAIT	965	All Points	541	UNITED		
All Points	*	SAUDI ARABIA	966	KINGDOM	44	
LIECHTENSTEIN	41	Jeddah	21	Belfast	232	
All Points	75	Khamis Mushait	7	Birmingham	21	
LUXEMBOURG	352	Mecca	22	Bradford	274	
All Points	*	Medina	41	Bristol	272	
MALAYSIA	60	Riyadh	1	Coventry	203	
Alor Star	4	SINGAPORE	65	Edinburgh	31	
Baranang	3	All Points	*	Glasgow	41	
Ipoh	5	SOUTH AFRICA	27	Leeds	532	
Kuala Lumpur	3	Cape Town	21	Leicester	533	
MONACO	33	Durban	31	Liverpool	51	
All Points	93	Johannesburg	11	London	1	
NETHERLANDS	31	Pretoria	12	Manchester	61	
Amsterdam	20	SPAIN	34	Nottingham	602	
Eindhoven	40	Barcelona	3	Sheffield	742	
Haarlem	23	Madrid	1	Southampton	703	
Rotterdam	10	Valencia	6	VATICAN CITY	39	
The Hague	70	SWEDEN	46	All Points	6	
Utrecht	30	Goteborg	31	VENEZUELA	58	
NETHERLANDS		Norrkoping	11	Barquisimeto	51	
ANTILLES	599	Stockholm	8	Caracas	2	
Bonaire	7	Uppsala	18	Maracaibo	61	
Curacao	9	SWITZERLAND	41	Maracay	43	
Saba	4	Basel	61	Valencia	41	
NEW ZEALAND	64	Bern	31	YUGOSLAVIA	38	
Auckland	9	Geneva	22	Belgrade	11	
Christchurch	3	Lausanne	21	Sarajevo	71	
Dunedin	24	Zurich	1	Skoplje	91	
Wellington	4	TAHITI	689	Zagreb	41	
NICARAGUA	505	All Points	*			
Granada	72	THAILAND	66			
Leon	31	Bangkok	2			
Managua	2	TURKEY	90			
NORWAY	47	Ankara	41			
Bergen	5	Istanbul	1			

*No city code required

TOLL-FREE TRAVEL

AIRLINES	800 TOLL-FREE NUMBER	ATLANTA	CHICAGO
Aer Lingus Irish	223-6537		312 236-7808
Aéroflot			
Aerolineas Argentinas	327-0276		312 951-1944
Aeromexico		800 227-6639	800 223-9780
AeroPeru	255-7378		
Air Canada	422-6232		
Air Florida	292-2121		
Air France	237-2747		312 440-7922
Air India	223-7776	404 955-6662	312 782-6263
Air Jamaica	523-5585		
Air New Zealand	262-1234	800 282-1234	
Air Panama International			312 631-7803
Alaska Airlines	426-0333	800 426-5606	
Alitalia	223-5730	404 393-9550	312 427-4720
American		404 521-2655	312 372-8000
Avianca	327-9899	404 634-1101	
Aviateca International			312 939-3873
Bahamas Air	222-4262	404 321-0331	
British Airways	247-9297	800 247-9297	312 686-5700
B.W.I.A. International	327-7401		
CP Air	426-7000		
Capitol Air	227-4865		
China Airlines	227-5118		312 427-2920
Continental	231-0856	404 436-3300	312 686-6500
Czechoslovak (CSA) Air Lines			
Delta Air Lines	523-7777	404 765-5000	312 346-5300
Eastern Air Lines	327-8376	404 435-1111	312 467-2900
Ecuatoriana Airlines	328-2367		312 332-0063
El Al Israel Airlines	223-6700		312 686-0616
Ethiopian Airlines		404 588-9476	312 663-4100
Finnair	223-5700	404 547-4449	312 296-1144
Frontier Airlines			800 255-5050
Gulf Air			
Hawaiian Airlines	367-5320	404 294-4300	312 699-6820

TOLL-FREE TRAVEL

Airlines	Los Angeles	New York	Washington, D.C.
Aer Lingus Irish		212 557-1110	
Aéroflot			202 429-4922
Aerolineas Argentinas	213 623-4490	212 974-3300	
Aeromexico	213 237-6639	212 391-2900	800 227-6639
AeroPeru	213 448-0515	212 972-5855	
Air Canada	213 776-7171	212 869-1900	202 638-3348
Air Florida			
Air France	213 625-7171	212 247-0100	202 337-8711
Air India	213 380-4481	212 751-6200	202 785-8989
Air Jamaica	800 523-5585	212 310-0800	
Air New Zealand	213 642-0196	212 661-7444	
Air Panama	213 661-6286	212 246-4033	202 659-9581
International			
Alaska Airlines	800 426-0333		
Alitalia		212 582-8900	202 393-2829
American	213 935-6045	212 431-1132	202 393-2345
Avianca	213 626-9147	212 246-5241	
Aviateca International			
Bahamas Air		212 947-3440	
British Airways	213 748-2275	212 983-6875	202 471-4520
B.W.I.A. International		212 581-3200	
CP Air	213 626-4508		
Capitol Air		212 883-0740	
China Airlines	213 624-1161	212 399-7877	202 833-1760
Continental	213 772-6000	718 565-1100	202 478-9700
Czechoslovak (CSA)		212 682-5833	
Air Lines			
Delta Air Lines	213 386-5510	212 239-0700	202 468-2282
Eastern Air Lines	213 380-2070	(D) 212 986-5000	202 393-4000
		(I) 212 661-3500	
Ecuatoriana Airlines	213 627-8844	212 399-1180	202 296-3129
El Al Israel Airlines		212 486-2600	203 296-5440
Ethiopian Airlines	213 462-7291	212 867-0095	202 363-0207
Finnair	213 623-7171	212 889-7070	202 659-8233
Frontier Airlines	213 617-3606		
Gulf Air		212 563-7725	
Hawaiian Airlines		212 355-4843	

TOLL-FREE TRAVEL

AIRLINES	800 TOLL-FREE NUMBER	ATLANTA	CHICAGO
Iberia Air Lines of Spain	221-9741	404 266-3481	312 332-0694
Icelandair	223-5390	800 223-5500	312 694-4133
Japan Air Lines	525-3663		312 565-7000
KLM Royal Dutch Airlines	556-7777	404 523-5900	312 861-9300
Korean Airlines		404 522-7461	312 558-9300
Kuwait Airways			312 437-5455
Lot Polish Airlines			312 236-3388
Lufthansa German Airlines	645-3880	404 266-1616	312 751-0111
Mexicana Airlines	531-7921	404 231-3587	312 346-8414
Midway Airlines	621-5700		312 767-3400
Northwest		(D) 404 762-5561	(D) 312 346-4900
		(I) 800 447-4747	(I) 312 346-6570
Olympic Airways	223-1226		312 329-0400
Ozark Air Lines		404 688-9565	312 558-7000
Pakistan International			312 263-3082
Pan Am	221-1111	404 524-8900	312 686-3770
Philippine Airlines	435-9725		312 332-7477
Qantas Airways	227-4500		312 686-7942
Republic Airlines	328-2213	404 762-5561	312 346-9860
Sabena Belgian World Airlines	521-0135	800 223-0470	800 645-3790
SAS Scandinavian Airlines	221-2350		312 855-3900
Singapore Airlines	742-3333	404 577-5644	312 332-3780
Swissair		404 956-0251	
TAP The Airline of Portugal	221-7370		
Trans Australia Airlines	227-4500		312 565-0803
Trans World Airlines		404 522-5738	(D) 312 558-7000
			(I) 312 332-1118
United Airlines		404 394-2234	312 569-3000
USAir		800 428-4322	312 726-1201
Varig Brazilian Airlines	468-2744		312 565-1301
Viasa Airways	327-5454		
Yugoslav (JAT) Airlines			312 782-1322

TOLL-FREE TRAVEL

AIRLINES	LOS ANGELES	NEW YORK	WASHINGTON, D.C.
Iberia Air Lines of Spain		718 793-3300	202 293-1453
Icelandair	800 223-5500	212 967-8888	800 223-5500
Japan Air Lines	213 620-9580	212 838-4400	800 525-3663
KLM Royal Dutch Airlines	213 776-6300	212 759-3600	
Korean Airlines	213 484-1900	212 371-4820	800 223-1155
Kuwait Airways	213 627-1485	212 308-5454	202 296-4644
Lot Polish Airlines		212 869-1074	
Lufthansa German Airlines	213 680-0700	718 895-1277	202 296-5604
Mexicana Airlines	213 646-9500	212 687-0388	202 371-6400
Midway Airlines		212 532-5050	800 621-5700
Northwest	(D) 213 380-1511	(D) 212 736-1220	(D) 202 737-7333
	(I) 213 383-5480	(I) 212 563-7200	(I) 202 737-7190
Olympic Airways	213 624-6441	212 838-3600	202 659-2511
Ozark Air Lines		212 732-3286	
Pakistan International		212 370-9158	202 737-0037
Pan Am	213 639-7440	212 687-2600	202 845-8000
Philippine Airlines		212 575-7850	202 331-8950
Qantas Airways	800 622-0850	212 764-0200	202 223-3030
Republic Airlines	213 638-4101	212 581-8851	202 347-0448
Sabena Belgian World Airlines		212 936-7800	800 645-3700
SAS Scandinavian Airlines	213 655-8600	718 657-7700	202 833-2424
Singapore Airlines	213 655-9270	212 949-9098	202 466-3747
Swissair	213 410-9452	718 995-8400	202 296-5380
TAP The Airline of Portugal	800 221-7370	212 944-2100	800 221-7370
Trans Australia Airlines	213 626-2352	800 227-4500	
Trans World Airlines	(D) 213 484-2244	(D) 212 290-2121	(D) 202 737-7400
	(I) 213 484-9319	(I) 212 290-2141	(I) 202 737-7404
United Airlines	213 772-2121	718 803-2200	202 893-3400
USAir	800 428-4322	212 736-3200	202 783-4500
Varig Brazilian Airlines	213 776-1421	212 682-3100	202 331-8913
Viasa Airways	800 327-5454	212 581-9799	800 221-2150
Yugoslav (JAT) Airlines	213 388-0379	212 765-4050	202 822-9449

METRIC CONVERSION

METRIC CONVERSION TABLES

LINEAR	1 inch = 2.54 centimeters 1 foot = 30.48 centimeters 1 yard = .914 meter 1 mile = 1.610 kilometers	1 millimeter = .03937 inch 1 centimeter = .3937 inch 1 meter = 3.2808 feet = 1.0936 yard 1 kilometer = .621 mile
AREA	1 acre = .4047 hectares	1 hectare = 2.4711 acres
WEIGHT	1 ounce = 28.3495 grams 1 pound = .4536 kilograms 1 ton = 907.18 kilograms	1 gram = .035 ounce 1 kilogram = 2.204 pounds 1 metric ton = 1.1023 tons
VOLUME	1 ounce = 29.58 milliliters 1 quart = .9464 liter 1 gallon = 3.7854 liters 1 cubic inch = 16.39 cubic centimeters 1 cubic foot = .0283 cubic meter 1 cubic yard = .7646 cubic meter	1 milliliter = .0348 ounce 1 liter = 1.0567 quarts 1 liter = .2642 gallon 1 cubic centimeter = .0610 cubic inch 1 cubic meter = 35.315 cubic feet 1 cubic meter = 1.3080 cubic yards

TEMPERATURE

To convert Celsius into Fahrenheit:
Multiply Celsius degrees by 9, divide by 5, add 32.

To convert Fahrenheit into Celsius:
Subtract 32 from degrees of Fahrenheit and multiply by 5, then divide by 9.

Water freezes	32° F	0° C
Water boils	212° F	100° C
Absolute zero	−459.6° F	−273.1° C

F = Fahrenheit
C = Celsius (also known as Centigrade)

WEATHER

F	C
110	43
100	37.8
90	32.2
80	26.7
70	21.1
60	15.6
50	10
40	4.4
32	0
20	−6.7
10	−12.2
0	−17.8
−10	−23.3
−20	−28.9

FEVER

F	C.
105	40.5
104	40
103	39.4
102	38.8
101	38.3
100	37.7
98.6	37
(normal)	(normal)
97	36.1

EQUIVALENT SIZES

WOMEN'S SIZES

WOMEN'S COATS, SUITS, DRESSES, SKIRTS, SLACKS, SWEATERS & BLOUSES

American	6	8	10	12	14	16
British	8	10	12	14	16	18
Continental	38	40	42	44	46	48

SHOES

American	4½	5½	6½	7½	8½	9½
British	3	4	5	6	7	8
Continental	36	37	38	39	40	41

MEN'S SIZES

MEN'S COATS, SUITS, SLACKS, SWEATERS & SHIRTS

American	36	38	40	42	44	46	48
British	36	38	40	42	44	46	48
Continental	46	48	50	52	54	56	58

SHOES

American	7½	8½	9½	10½	11½	12½	13½
British	7	8	9	10	11	12	13
Continental	41	42	43	44	46	47	48

MEN'S SHIRTS (COLLAR SIZES)

US/UK (in.)	15	15½	16	16½	17	17½
Europe (cm)	38	39½	41	42	43	44

STATE TOURIST OFFICES

ALABAMA
Bureau of Tourism & Travel
532 S. Perry St.
Montgomery, AL 36104
205-261-4169 or
1-800-ALABAMA (our of
state
1-800-392-8096 (in state)

ALASKA
Alaska Division of Tourism
P.O. Box E
Juneau, AK 99811
907-465-2010

ARIZONA
Arizona Office of Tourism
1100 West Washington
Phoenix, AZ 85007
602-255-3618

ARKANSAS
Arkansas Department of
Parks and Tourism
1 Capitol Mall
Little Rock, AR 72201
501-682-7777 or
1-800-482-8999 or
1-800-643-8383
(out of state)

CALIFORNIA
California Office of Tourism
Department of Commerce
1121 L Street
Suite 103
Sacramento, CA 95814
916-322-2881

COLORADO
Colorado Tourism Board
1625 Broadway, Suite 1700
Denver, CO 80202
303-592-5410
For a vacation planning kit,
call Toll-free 1-800-433-2656

CONNECTICUT
Tourism Promotion Service
Connecticut Department of
Economic Development
210 Washington St.
Hartford, CT 06106
203-566-3948 or
1-800-842-7492
(Connecticut)
1-800-243-1685 (Maine
through Virginia)

DELAWARE
Delaware Tourism Office
Delaware Development Office
99 Kings Highway
P.O. Box 1401
Dover, DE 19903
302-736-4271 or
1-800-441-8846

DISTRICT OF COLUMBIA
Washington Convention and
Visitors Association
Suite 250
1575 Eye Street, NW
Washington, D.C. 20005
202-789-7000

FLORIDA
Department of Commerce
Visitors Inquiry
126 Van Buren St.
Tallahassee, FL 32399-2000
904-487-1462

GEORGIA
Tourist Division
P.O. Box 1776
Atlanta, GA 30301
404-656-3590 or
1-800-VISIT-GA

HAWAII
Hawaii Visitors Bureau
2270 Kalakaua Ave., Suite 801
Honolulu, HI 96815
808-923-1811

IDAHO
Department of Commerce
700 W. State St.
Second Floor
Boise, ID 83720
208-334-2470 or
1-800-635-7820

ILLINOIS
Illinois Department of Commerce and Community Affairs,
Office of Tourism
620 East Adams Street
Springfield, IL 62701
217-782-7139

INDIANA
Indiana Dept. of Commerce
Tourism Division
1 North Capitol, Suite 700
Indianapolis, IN 46204
317-232-8860

IOWA
Iowa Department of Economic
Development
Bureau of Tourism and Visitors
200 East Grand Avenue
Des Moines, IA 50309
515-281-3100

KANSAS
Travel & Tourism Development
Division
Department of Commerce
400 W. 8th St., 5th Floor
Topeka, KS 66603
913-296-2009

KENTUCKY
Department of Travel
Development
Capital Plaza Tower
Frankfort, KY 40601
502-564-4930 or
1-800-225-TRIP
(Continental United States and
provinces of Ontario and
Quebec, Canada)

LOUISIANA
Office of Tourism
P.O. Box 94291
Baton Rouge, LA 70804-9291
504-342-8119 or
1-800-33GUMBO

MAINE
Maine Publicity Bureau
97 Winthrop St., P.O. Box 2300
Hallowell, ME 04347-2300
207-289-2423

MARYLAND
Office of Tourist Development
217 E. Redwood St.
Baltimore, MD 21202
301-974-3517

MASSACHUSETTS
Dept. of Food & Agriculture
Bureau of Markets
100 Cambridge St.
Boston, MA 02202
617-727-3018

MICHIGAN
Travel Bureau
Department of Commerce
P.O. Box 30226
Lansing, MI 48909
1-800-5432-YES
or for latest recorded information
on special seasonal activities,
1-800-292-5404 (in-state) or
1-800-248-5708 (out-of-state):
CT, DC, DE, IA, IL, IN, KY,
MA, MD, MN, MO, NC, NH,
NJ, NY, OH, PA, RI, SD, TN,
VA, VT, WI, WV

MINNESOTA
Minnesota Office of Tourism
375 Jackson St.
250 Skyway Level
Farm Credit Services Bldg.
St. Paul, MN 55101
612-296-5029 or
1-800-328-1461 (U.S. Toll-Free)
and (Minnesota Toll-Free)
1-800-652-9747

MISSISSIPPI
Division of Tourism
Department of Economic
Development
P.O. Box 849
Jackson, MS 39205
601-359-3414 or
1-800-647-2290

MISSOURI
Missouri Division of Tourism
Truman State Office Bldg.
301 W. High St.
P.O. Box 1055
Jefferson City, MO 65102
314-751-4133

MONTANA
Travel Montana
Department of Commerce
1424 9th Ave.
Helena, MT 59620
406-444-2654 or
1-800-541-1447

STATE TOURIST OFFICES

NEBRASKA
Dept. of Economic Development
Division of Travel and Tourism
301 Centennial Mall South
P.O. Box 94666
Lincoln, NE 68509
402-471-3796 or
  1-800-742-7595 or
  1-800-228-4307 (out-of-state)

NEVADA
Commission on Tourism
Capitol Complex
Carson City, NV 89710
1-800-Nevada-8

NEW HAMPSHIRE
Office of Vacation Travel
P.O. Box 856
Concord, NH 03301
603-271-2666
  or for recorded weekly events,
  ski conditions, foliage reports
  1-800-258-3608

NEW JERSEY
Division of Travel and Tourism
CN-826
Trenton, NJ 08625
609-292-2470

NEW MEXICO
New Mexico Tourism & Travel
  Division ED & TD
Room 119, Joseph M. Montoya
  Bldg.
1100 St. Francis Dr.
Santa Fe, NM 87503
505-827-0291 or
  1-800-545-2040

NEW YORK
Division of Tourism
1 Commerce Plaza
Albany, NY 12245
Toll free from all continental
  states, Puerto Rico, and the
  Virgin Islands
1-800-225-5697 or
518-474-4116

NORTH CAROLINA
Travel and Tourism Division
Department of Commerce
430 North Salisbury St.
Raleigh, NC 27611
919-733-4171 or 1-800-VISIT NC

NORTH DAKOTA
North Dakota Tourism
  Promotion
Liberty Memorial Building
Capitol Grounds
Bismarck, ND 58505
701-224-2525 or
  1-800-437-2077 (out-of-state)

OHIO
Ohio Division of Travel and
  Tourism
P.O. Box 1001
Columbus, OH 43266-0101
614-466-8844 (Business Office)
  1-800-BUCKEYE (National
  Toll-Free Travel Hotline)

OKLAHOMA
Oklahoma Tourism and
  Recreation Dept.
Literature Distribution Center
215 NE 28th Street
Oklahoma City, OK 73105
405-521-2409 (in Oklahoma &
  states not mentioned below)
  1-800-652-6552 (in AR, CO,
  KS, MO, NM, and TX except
  area code 512)

OREGON
Tourism Division
Oregon Economic Development
595 Cottage St., NE
Salem, OR 97310
503-378-3451 or
  1-800-547-7842 (out-of-state)

PENNSYLVANIA
Bureau of Travel Development
453 Forum Building
Harrisburg, PA 17120
717-787-5453 (Business Office)
  1-800-VISIT PA, ext. 275
  (Consumer information)

RHODE ISLAND
Rhode Island Tourism Division
7 Jackson Walkway
Providence, RI 02903
401-277-2601 or
  1-800-556-2484 (For residents
  from Maine to Virginia/
  West Virginia and Northern
  Ohio)

SOUTH CAROLINA
South Carolina Division of
  Tourism
Box 71
Columbia, SC 29202
803-734-0122

SOUTH DAKOTA
Department of Tourism
Capitol Lake Plaza
Pierre, South Dakota 57501
605-773-3301 or
  1-800-843-1930 out of SD;
  1-800-952-2217 in SD

TENNESSEE
Department of Tourist
  Development
P.O. Box 23170
Nashville, TN 37202
615-741-2158

TEXAS
Travel Information Services
State Highway Department
P.O. Box 5064
Austin, TX 78763-5064
512-463-8971

UTAH
Utah Travel Council
Council Hall, Capitol Hill
Salt Lake City, UT 84114
801-538-1030

VERMONT
Agency of Development and
  Community Affairs
Travel Division
134 State St.
Montpelier, VT 05602
802-828-3236

VIRGINIA
Virginia Division of Tourism
202 North Ninth Street
Suite 500
Richmond, VA 23219
804-786-4484

WASHINGTON
Washington State Dept. of Trade
  and Economic Development
101 General Administration
  Bldg. AX-13
Olympia, WA 98504
206-753-5630

WASHINGTON, D.C.
See District of Columbia

WEST VIRGINIA
Dept. of Commerce
State Capitol Complex
Charleston, WV 25305
304-348-2286 or
  1-800-CALL-WVA

WISCONSIN
Department of Development
Division of Tourism
  Development
Box 7606
Madison, WI 53707
Toll free in WI and neighbor
  states 1-800-escapes
others: 608-266-2161

WYOMING
Wyoming Travel Commission
I-25 at College Drive
Cheyenne, WY 82002-0660
307-777-7777 or
  1-800-225-5996

U.S. CONSULATES

Austria	Vienna: A-1091, Boltzmanngasse 16. Tel. (222) 31-55-11
Brazil	Rio de Janeiro: Avenida Presidente Wilson. Tel. (021) 292-7117
Belgium	Brussels: 22 Blvd. du Regent. Tel. (02) 513-3830
Canada	Ottawa: 100 Wellington St. Tel. (613) 238-5335
China	Beijing: Guang Hua Lu 17. Tel. 52-2033
Colombia	Bogota: Calle 38, No. 8-61. Tel. 285-1300
Denmark	Copenhagen: Dag Hammarskjolds Alie 24. Tel. (01) 42-31-44
Egypt	Cairo: 5 Sharia Latin America. Tel. 28219
Finland	Helsinki: Itainen Puistotie 15-A. Tel. 171931
France	Paris: 2 Avenue Gabriel. Tel. 296-1202
Germany	Berlin: Ciayalee 170. Tel. (030) 83240-87
	Munich: Koeniginstrasse 5. Tel. (089) 23011
Great Britain	London, England: 24/31 Grosvenor Sq. Tel. (01) 499-9000
Greece	Athens: 91 Vasilissis Sophias Blvd. Tel. 721-2951
Honduras	Tegucigalpa: Avenida La Paz. Tel. 721-2951
Hong Kong	26 Garden Road. Tel. 239011
India	New Delhi: Shanti Path, Chanakyapuri. Tel. 600651
Ireland	Dublin: 42 Elgin Rd., Ballsbridge. Tel. 6887777
Israel	Tel Aviv: 71 Hayarkon St. Tel. (03) 654338
	Jerusalem: 18 Agron Rd. Tel. (02) 234271
Italy	Rome: Via Veneto 119/A. Tel. (6) 4674
Japan	Tokyo: 10-1, Akasaka 1-Chome, Minato-Ku. Tel. 583-7141
Kenya	Nairobi: Moi/Haile Selassie Ave. Tel. 334141
Mexico	Mexico City: D.F., Paseo de la Reforma 305. Tel. (905) 21-1-0042
Netherlands	The Hague: Lange Voorhout 102. Tel. (070) 62-49-11
Norway	Oslo: Drammensvein 18. Tel. 44-85-50
Philippines	Manila: 1201 Roxas Blvd. Tel. 521-7116
Portugal	Lisbon: Avenida das Forcas Armadas, 1600. Tel. 72-5600
Saudi Arabia	Riyadh: Sulaimaniah District. Tel. (01) 464-0012
Spain	Madrid: Serrano, 75. Tel. 276-3400
Sweden	Stockholm: Strandvagen 101. Tel. (08) 63-05-20
Switzerland	Geneva: 11, Route de Pregny. Tel. (022) 990211
Turkey	Ankara: 110 Ataturk Blvd. Tel. 26-54-70
Venezuela	Caracas: Avenida Francisco de Miranda. Tel. 284-7111
Yugoslavia	Belgrade: Kneza Milosa 50. Tel. (011) 645-655

FIRST AID

WHAT TO DO IN AN EMERGENCY

HELP THE VICTIM

1. **Rescue the Victim** from life-threatening danger, if necessary.

2. **Send Someone** to seek medical help, if the injury or illness is serious.

3. **Restore or Maintain Breathing and Heartbeat** using mouth-to-mouth resuscitation or CPR.

4. **Control Heavy Bleeding** by applying a clean compress and firm, direct pressure to the wound.

5. **Treat Poisoning** as directed by the Poison Control Center. Save any container and try to identify the poison before calling the Center.

6. **Prevent Shock** by helping the victim to lie down and by maintaining body temperature.

7. **Examine the Victim** for other injuries.

8. **Seek Medical Help**. Call 911, if not done previously. Arrange follow-up medical care.

9. **Keep Checking** the victim's breathing and pulse. Don't leave until medical help arrives.

GET EMERGENCY MEDICAL HELP FAST

While one person administers first aid or CPR to the victim, another must seek medical help.

Dial 911 or the emergency number for your area. Be ready to answer questions and provide important information.

Location of the Emergency including cross streets, floor and room numbers, and the phone number from which you are calling.

What Happened? What kind of accident, injury, or illness occurred?

How Many People Need Help? Is anyone bleeding or unconscious? What first aid has been administered?

Don't Hang Up First! Be sure you have provided all necessary information.

Training in first aid and CPR can save a life. Learn it BEFORE you need it by contacting your Red Cross chapter.

WHEN BREATHING STOPS

1. Check for unresponsiveness—Tap or gently shake victim. Shout "Are you o.k.?"

2. Shout, "Help!"—Get attention of people who can phone for help.

3. Position the victim on his or her back—roll the victim toward you by pulling slowly and evenly from the victim's hip and shoulder.

4. Open the airway—Tilt the head back and lift chin with fingers under bony part of jaw.

5. Check for breathlessness— Look, listen and feel for breathing for 3 to 5 seconds.

6. Give two full breaths—Keep head tilted back. Pinch nose. Seal your mouth tightly around the victim's mouth. Give two full breaths for 1 to 1½ seconds each.

7. Check for pulse at the side of the neck—Keep head tilted back. Feel for carotid pulse for 5 to 10 seconds.

8. Phone EMS System for help —Send someone to phone for an ambulance. Send 2 people if possible. Give location of emergency and condition of victim.

9. Begin rescue breathing— Keep head tilted back. Pinch nose. Give 1 breath every 5 seconds. Look, listen and feel between breaths.

10. Recheck pulse every minute —Keep head tilted back. Feel for carotid pulse for 5 to 10 seconds. If the victim has pulse but is not breathing, continue rescue breathing.

FIRST AID FOR CHOKING

1. Ask "Are you choking?" If victim cannot breathe, cough or speak . . .

2. Give the Heimlich Maneuver:
   a) Stand behind the victim.
   b) Wrap your arms around the victim's waist.
   c) Make a fist with one hand. Place your fist (thumbside) against the victim's stomach in the midline just

ABOVE THE NAVEL AND WELL BELOW THE RIB MARGIN.
   d) Grasp your fist with your other hand.
   e) PRESS INTO STOMACH WITH A QUICK UP- WARD THRUST.

3. Repeat if necessary.

4. If a victim has become un- conscious—Sweep the mouth.

5. Attempt rescue breathing.

6. Give 6–10 abdominal thrusts. Repeat steps 4, 5, and 6 as necessary.

EQUIPPING A FIRST AID KIT

- 2 packages of 1″ adhesive compress
- 2 packages of 1″ bandage compress
- 1 package of 3″ bandage com- press
- 1 package of 4″ bandage com- press
- 1 package of 3″ × 3″ plain gauze pads
- 1 package of 2″ gauze roller bandage
- 2 packages of plain absorbent gauze (one half square yard)
- 2 packages of plain absorbent gauze (24″ by 72″)
- 3 packages of triangular ban- dages (40″ tourniquet)
- Scissors, Tweezers, and Eye Dressing packet

You can add items suited to your own needs and based on your doctor's advice. Most impor- tantly you should take a course in first aid so that you know how to use your first aid kit.

PHRASE GUIDE

ENGLISH	FRENCH
Yes	Oui
No	Non
Please	S'il vous plaît
Thank you	Merci
Good morning	Bonjour
Good evening	Bonsoir
Good-bye	Au revoir
How do you do? (Pleased to meet you.)	Enchanté(e)
How are you?	Comment allez-vous?
I beg your pardon.	Pardon
Do you speak English?	Parlez-vous anglais?
Please write it down.	Ecrivez-le, s'il vous plaît.
Can you tell me . . . ?	Pouvez-vous me dire . . . ?
Can you help me?	Pouvez-vous m'aider?
I'm looking for . . .	Je cherche . . .
I'm hungry.	J'ai faim.
I'm thirsty.	J'ai soif.
I'm tired.	Je suis fatigué(e).
I'm lost.	Je me suis perdu(e).
It's very important.	C'est très important.

ENGLISH	SPANISH
Yes	Sí
No	No
Please	Por favor
Thank you	Gracias
Good morning	Buenos días
Good evening	Buenas tardes
Good-bye	Adiós
How do you do? (Pleased to meet you.)	Encantado(a) de conocerie
How are you?	¿Como esta usted?
I beg your pardon.	Perdóneme
Do you speak English?	¿Habla usted Inglès?
Please write it down.	Por favor, escríbalo.
Can you tell me . . . ?	¿Puede usted decirme?
Can you help me?	¿Puede usted ayudarme?
I'm looking for . . .	Estoy buscando . . .
I'm hungry.	Tengo hambre.
I'm thirsty.	Tengo sed.
I'm tired.	Esto cansado(a).
I'm lost.	Me he perdido.
It's important.	Es importante.

PHRASE GUIDE

ENGLISH	ITALIAN
Yes	Sí
No	No
Please	Per favore
Thank you	Grazie
Good morning	Buon giorno
Good evening	Buona sera
Good-bye	Arrivederci
How do you do? (Pleased to meet you.)	Molte lieto(a).
How are you?	Come sta?
I beg your pardon.	Prego
Do you speak English?	Parla inglese?
Please write it down.	Per favore, me lo scriva.
Can you tell me . . . ?	Può dirmi . . . ?
Can you help me?	Può aiutarmi?
I'm looking for . . .	Cerco . . .
I'm hungry.	Ho fame.
I'm thirsty.	Ho sete.
I'm tired.	Sono stanco(a).
I'm lost.	Mi sono perduto(a).
It's important.	È importante.

ENGLISH	GERMAN
Yes	Ja
No	Nein
Please	Bitte
Thank you	Danke
Good morning	Guten Morgen
Good evening	Guten Abend
Good-bye	Auf Wiedersehen
How do you do? (Pleased to meet you.)	Sehr erfreut.
How are you?	Wie geht es ihnen?
I beg your pardon.	Wie bitte?
Do you speak English?	Sprechen Sie Englisch?
Please write it down.	Schreiben Sie es bitte auf.
Can you tell me . . . ?	Können Sie mir sagen . . . ?
Can you help me?	Können Sie mir helfen?
I'm looking for . . .	Ich suche . . .
I'm hungry.	Ich habe Hunger.
I'm thirsty.	Ich habe Durst.
I'm tired.	Ich bin müde.
I'm lost.	Ich habe mich verirrt.
It's important.	Es ist wichtig.

ADDRESSES

Name _____

Address _____

Telephone # _____

Name _____

Address _____

Telephone # _____

Name _____

Address _____

Telephone # _____

Name _____

Address _____

Telephone # _____

Name _____

Address _____

Telephone # _____

Name _____

Address _____

Telephone # _____

ADDRESSES

Name _____

Address _____

Telephone # _____

Name _____

Address _____

Telephone # _____

Name _____

Address _____

Telephone # _____

Name _____

Address _____

Telephone # _____

Name _____

Address _____

Telephone # _____

Name _____

Address _____

Telephone # _____

ADDRESSES

Name _____

Address _____

Telephone # _____

Name _____

Address _____

Telephone # _____

Name _____

Address _____

Telephone # _____

Name _____

Address _____

Telephone # _____

Name _____

Address _____

Telephone # _____

Name _____

Address _____

Telephone # _____

ADDRESSES

Name _____

Address _____

Telephone # _____

Name _____

Address _____

Telephone # _____

Name _____

Address _____

Telephone # _____

Name _____

Address _____

Telephone # _____

Name _____

Address _____

Telephone # _____

Name _____

Address _____

Telephone # _____

ADDRESSES

Name _____

Address _____

Telephone # _____

Name _____

Address _____

Telephone # _____

Name _____

Address _____

Telephone # _____

Name _____

Address _____

Telephone # _____

Name _____

Address _____

Telephone # _____

Name _____

Address _____

Telephone # _____

ADDRESSES

Name _____

Address _____

Telephone # _____

Name _____

Address _____

Telephone # _____

Name _____

Address _____

Telephone # _____

Name _____

Address _____

Telephone # _____

Name _____

Address _____

Telephone # _____

Name _____

Address _____

Telephone # _____

ADDRESSES

Name ———————————————————

Address ———————————————————

Telephone # ———————————————————

Name ———————————————————

Address ———————————————————

Telephone # ———————————————————

Name ———————————————————

Address ———————————————————

Telephone # ———————————————————

Name ———————————————————

Address ———————————————————

Telephone # ———————————————————

Name ———————————————————

Address ———————————————————

Telephone # ———————————————————

Name ———————————————————

Address ———————————————————

Telephone # ———————————————————